HUMAN to
HORSEMAN

HUMAN to
HORSEMAN

A Journey of Discovery,
Growth, and Celebration

RICK LAMB

Foreword by CHERRY HILL

T
Trafalgar Square
North Pomfret, Vermont

First published in 2008 by
Trafalgar Square Books
North Pomfret, Vermont 05053

Printed in the USA

Library of Congress Cataloging-in-Publication Data

Lamb, Richard A.
  Human to horseman : a journey of discovery, growth, and celebration / Rick Lamb.
    p. cm.
  ISBN 978-1-57076-394-6
  1. Horsemanship. 2. Lamb, Richard A. I. Title.
  SF309.L18 2008
  798.2--dc22
                          2007049303

Photo credits: Coco (Photos 1, 26); Diana Lamb (Photos 2, 6, 7, 8, 9, 10, 13, 15, 16, 18, 19, 23, 27);
Al Raitano (Photo 3); Susan Bolin (Photo 4); Courtesy of the Rick Lamb Collection (Photos 5, 12,
17, 20, 21, 25); Rick Lamb (Photos 11, 14); Debby Miller (Photo 22); Heidi Nyland (Photo 24)

The quotes on pp. 73 and 107 are from *The Revolution in Horsemanship* and *What It Means to
Mankind* by Robert M. Miller, DVM, and Rick Lamb (2005), reprinted by permission from
Lyons Press.

Book text and jacket design by Heather Mansfield
Typefaces: Warnock Pro, Gill Sans

10 9 8 7 6 5 4 3 2 1

THIS BOOK IS DEDICATED TO MY
LISTENERS, VIEWERS, AND READERS.
WITHOUT YOU, MY JOURNEY WOULD
BE VERY DIFFERENT AND NOT
NEARLY AS MUCH FUN.

CONTENTS

ACKNOWLEDGMENTS

Many people have influenced me in a positive way during my life and thus share a measure of credit for anything worthwhile that I accomplish.

Foremost would be my parents, Dick and Ann Lamb, of Wichita, Kansas. They did a remarkable job of guiding a young man with interests very different from their own.

Then there's my wife, Diana. I couldn't ask for a better friend, partner, cheerleader, and, when I need it most, critic.

My children—Ryan, Todd, and Blair—have quietly inspired me to do my best at any task before me, and I do the same for them.

My dear friend, Cherry Hill, is an icon to all of us who write for the horse-loving public and I thank her for penning the foreword.

I'd also like to acknowledge the other horsemen and horsewomen who have shared their passion and knowledge with me over the years. Their ideas have become so intertwined with my own that giving proper credit is not always possible.

Finally, I'd like to thank Caroline Robbins, Martha Cook, and Rebecca Didier at Trafalgar Square Books for giving me the opportunity to tell my story.

FOREWORD

Cherry Hill

Horses can have a profound effect on humans. There's the horse-crazy young girl, the novice bit-by-the-bug, and the weekend horse lover. But a *horseman* is something else. A dyed-in-the-wool horseman is indistinguishable from his horses.

Horses can become woven so permanently into the fabric of our days that our life becomes all about the horse. I was born with horses in my soul. Since I was a young girl, I've pursued my vocation with purpose and passion. This has allowed me to meet a great number of generous horses and wonderful people.

When I first got a phone call from Rick Lamb in 1997, he was just starting up *The Horse Show* radio program. Although he was horseless, I could tell it was just a matter of time. He was a human waiting for a horse to happen.

It was a treat to be a guest on his show because he was eager to learn, enthusiastic, sincere, and had a great sense of humor. Talk flowed freely and the banter was spontaneous and natural. He was a pro. Who would have ever guessed that he was a shy guy forcing himself over the public speaking hurdle? Not me. But Rick reveals that and much more in this book.

As I read his spirited journey of the last twelve years, I applauded his honesty and humility, appreciated his generosity, admired his solid work ethic, and was engrossed by the details of the marker events on his path. His courage and desire to continually challenge himself really comes through. It's been said that we have to risk to win. To the true horseman, winning is learning and growing. Rick knows all about that.

Not one to stagnate or get too comfortable, Rick is out there constantly reinventing himself. He remains open-minded by interviewing people from many sectors of the horse business and presenting their ideas to his listeners, viewers, and readers. He delves but does not judge. That's very refreshing in a world where people can tend to put on blinders and become herdbound.

As part of his working day, Rick is privileged to talk to some of today's top horsemen and women. All the while, he's processing and distilling the ideas into his own horseman's philosophy. When you think about it, he's created a dream job for himself. Is he lucky? Well, yes. But his success is not due to luck. It's because of his enthusiasm, hard work, and dedication.

This book is Rick's personal narrative describing his evolution, which would be fun enough in itself. But it also contains salient points to ponder at the end of each chapter. We get a Who's Who, the inside scoop, and morals to the stories. This book talks about riding and horsekeeping, yes, but much more. It's also about personal growth, human failures and triumphs, and life's poignant moments.

Rick rounds up his favorite maxims, which, if we all took to heart, would result in fewer tangles and more harmony all around. Since you've picked up this book, I suspect you are somewhere on your path to becoming a horseman and will relate to Rick's journey and enjoy his stories and ideas. And, if you stay open-minded, you'll be free to grow in your own way and at your own rate because as Rick himself says, each horseman's journey is unique, personal, and ongoing.

With that, I'll head to the barn and see what my horses are going to teach me today.

It's all about the horses.

Cherry Hill
2008

PREFACE

During the months prior to publication, I went round and round trying to decide on the proper slant for this book. At first, I wanted it to be a roadmap, a how-to guide that would allow the reader to start at square one and follow my prescribed path to becoming a horseman.

Then, I realized two important things: One, the path is different for each of us, and two, there is no getting to the end. A Horseman—with a capital "H"—is an ideal of perfection to which we can all aspire but none can reach. Now, those are fine realizations but a book built around them would give the reader precious little to hang his or her hat on. I may not be able to provide a step-by-step guide that works for everyone, but I need to provide something of value in this practical matter of getting along with horses.

What I ended up with strikes, I hope, a good compromise. It's the story of the past dozen years of my life, a journey from a human ignorant of nearly everything about horses, except, of course, my own fascination with them, to a horseman striving to become a Horseman. It's a story that has played out on a public stage, a story complete with mistakes, missteps, and moments of insight. It is my hope that you will find it both entertaining and instructive.

But there's more than just my story in these pages. I will also tell you what I know with certainty, gleaned not only from my experience with horses, but from the experience of thousands of horse experts I've interviewed over the years. These are things I want you to burn into your brain. They are trustworthy. They are fact.

Finally, I have provided exercises, under the heading of Try This, at the end of each chapter. The vast majority of these do not require much effort, but if you take them seriously, they, too, well help you along on your journey.

Enjoy the ride!

Rick Lamb

1 A Cold Bleacher
The Journey Begins

Her name was Morgon and I didn't know her very well. We both worked at a video production center in north Phoenix—she as a traffic coordinator, and I as an independent audio contractor—and we both loved horses. When our paths crossed in that big building, the subject often came up. The year was 1995 and I was 44 years old.

"Rick, you have to see this," she said very matter-of-factly one day as she handed me a VHS tape. I figured it was a job that needed a voiceover, or sound effects, or a bit of music.

"He's doing a demo at Rawhide this Friday night," she explained. "It costs ten bucks, and if you don't think it was worth it, you come and tell me on Monday and I'll give you your money back." I still didn't know what she was talking about, but I took the tape and promised to watch it that evening.

A Glimpse of the Possibilities

The videotape introduced Pat Parelli, a tall, mustachioed California cowboy, and showed some pretty amazing things that he—and more impressively, his students—could do with horses. What I saw on the tape reminded me of trick horses I'd seen in the circus. But this was no circus and these were not performers. In fact, the students looked a lot like me, just regular folks with big smiles on their faces.

> What I saw on the tape reminded me of trick horses I'd seen in the circus.

I was intrigued. Although I'd never owned a horse, had very little riding experience, and knew almost nothing about the care and training of horses, I'd wanted horses in my life for as long as I could remember.

Diana, my wife, was always ready for a night out, so we hired a sitter for the kids and on Friday evening, drove out to Rawhide. Located at the north edge of Scottsdale, Phoenix's upscale suburb to the east, Rawhide was a busy tourist attraction, a tribute to a typical Old West town, complete with shootouts on the half hour and sarsaparilla on tap. At one end of the complex, there was an outdoor arena with lights, a sound system, and metal bleachers.

We made our way to the arena and I was surprised at the crowd that had gathered. Whether they were faithful followers or curious newbies like us I couldn't tell, but there was electricity in the air. It seemed that something special was about to happen.

It was late in the year, and although the Valley of the Sun is renowned for its mild winter days, evenings can get chilly. Within a few minutes of settling into our seats, I was thinking more about the cold bleachers than the hot demo I'd been promised.

The Demonstration

Finally, Pat came out and introduced himself to a round of polite applause. He stood in the arena and talked for the first half hour, saying things about horses I'd never heard before, about how they are prey animals and humans are predators, about how they communicate with body language, and about how normal horse handling techniques often frighten and confuse horses, and make them think of taking flight. He said it in an entertaining way that kept us all paying attention.

Pat said things about horses that I'd never heard before.

I took it in and tucked it away in my brain to think about later, when I wasn't so uncomfortable. But what happened next made me forget about the cold.

A teenaged girl, tall, wispy, and dark-haired, led her horse into the arena. The horse, a Saddlebred gelding, was agitated and oblivious to his owner, surging forward and pulling back, bumping into her, and calling out to other horses it smelled. I cringed, certain I was going to see the girl get hurt.

Pat introduced the girl and talked to her briefly about her horse, confirming that this horse had an issue with, among other things, loading in a trailer. For the first time, I noticed that a pickup with a straight-load, bumper-pull trailer had been positioned in the arena with its open back toward the audience. Pat asked the girl to try to load the horse and things got even uglier.

> The horse was oblivious to his owner, bumping into her and calling out to other horses.

"What an awful horse!" I thought to myself. I couldn't see that the horse was crying out for leadership. I couldn't see that it was behaving the only way it knew how, the way the girl or some other human had taught it. Finally, Pat released the girl and we all clapped for her, happy to see her away from the horse, and curious about what was going to happen next.

The horse had been outfitted with a knotted rope halter, something I'd never seen before. Attached to the halter was a thicker yachting rope that served as a lead line. Holding the lead rope casually in one hand, Pat turned his back on the horse and addressed the audience. It was a gutsy move that I felt certain was going to backfire on him.

> Without missing a beat in his speech, Pat kicked backward, striking the gelding hard in the middle of its chest.

Within seconds, the horse started crowding Pat the way it had crowded the girl. Then came a moment I will remember for all time. Without looking and without missing a beat in his speech, Pat kicked backward, striking the gelding hard in the middle of its chest. The audience gasped. We were as surprised as the horse. Here we had been listening to a philosophy that stressed understanding the horse and trying to see its point of view. Then suddenly the teacher was kicking the horse with all his might.

The horse instantly backed up two steps, head high and eyes wide. Pat continued talking and explained that his action was exactly what a more dominant horse would have done in a herd. He had barely gotten the words out before the horse had regrouped and was crowding him again.

Again, Pat's dusty boot found its mark, and again, the horse backed up a few steps. But this time, he also relaxed. His head came down, he let out a big sigh, and he licked his lips. From that moment forward, the horse kept a respectful distance and kept his attention on Pat, as though he was afraid he would miss something important if he looked away.

Horse Psychology

Pat went on to talk about leadership in the herd and how every horse must know who is in charge. It's part of the horse's survival mechanism.

Every horse must know who is in charge.

If a human does not show a horse that he is the leader in ways the horse understands, the horse is wired by Nature to take control of the team and assert his dominance over the human. That's how a lot of people get hurt, Pat said.

While I was processing all of this new information, Pat began to talk about trailer loading. He explained that it was natural for horses to be afraid to go into confined places because Nature had made them claustrophobic. Their instincts were to remain in open places where they could take flight instantly to escape danger. Pat's strategy would be to make the right thing—being inside the trailer—easy for the horse and the wrong thing—staying outside—difficult. That meant changing the mental association the horse made with the trailer. It made sense to me but I had no idea how Pat would get the job done.

He introduced a simple orange whip he called a Carrot Stick. He explained that he would use it as an extension of his arm, a way to touch the horse from a safe distance. He led the horse toward the trailer opening and when the horse refused to go any further, Pat pointed toward

The taps were light at first and, little by little, got heavier, always with an even rhythm.

the opening with the hand holding the lead rope and began tapping the horse on the rump with the Carrot Stick in the other hand. The taps were light at first and, little by little, got heavier, always with an even rhythm.

Finally, the horse took a single step forward. Pat stopped tapping instantly and changed to gently rubbing and scratching the horse with the stick. He gave the horse a moment to think about the lesson and then did the whole thing again. This time, the horse seemed to get the idea a little more quickly. Again, Pat rewarded the try by taking away the pressure.

That part was counter-intuitive to me. I probably would have kept right on tapping, trying to get an even bigger try. That was certainly the most direct approach and like most humans, I was accustomed to taking the direct approach.

For the next fifteen or twenty minutes, Pat worked with the horse, showing him that moving toward the trailer, and eventually into it, was always a better deal than staying outside. Pat created pressure, then rewarded the horse by removing the pressure. I noticed that the horse's progress wasn't perfectly linear. The horse sometimes did worse before he did better, moving every way except toward the trailer. But Pat stayed with the lesson, demonstrating what he called, "polite and passive persistence practiced in the proper position."

Eventually, the horse would willingly enter the trailer when Pat simply pointed him that direction and made the suggestion. It was the first of many times I would see a horse with a near-phobic feeling about entering a trailer have that attitude completely reversed with smart, patient training.

Natural Horsemanship

That evening opened my eyes to what Pat Parelli called, "natural" horsemanship. It wasn't English riding and it wasn't Western riding. It was more basic and more important than a riding discipline. It was about the horse's nature and how we could make it work for us rather than against us. I understood the idea. I liked it, and I decided that once my rear end thawed out, I would learn more. It was the beginning of a life-changing journey, a journey from human to Horseman.

> Natural horsemanship: It wasn't English riding and it wasn't Western riding. It was more basic and important than a riding discipline.

Insights

- Horsemanship transcends riding disciplines.

- A horse must know who the leader is.

- The human must be the leader.

- Horses are more likely to repeat behaviors that are rewarded.

- Releasing pressure is a reward to a horse.

- Horses are naturally claustrophobic.

- The natural tendencies of a horse can be changed with training.

TRY THIS

Observe Horses Being Horses

Take an afternoon off and go to a stable, farm, or ranch where you can watch a group of horses interacting with one another in a natural setting. Go alone. Take a lawn chair and make yourself comfortable. Clear your mind of distractions, and just observe for an hour or so. Try not to influence the horses in any way with your presence. Think about what you see.

2 **Thunder**
Discovering the Risk in Riding

After seeing Pat Parelli's demo, I was eager to begin my personal journey. But I had a pretty basic problem: I didn't own a horse. In anticipation of someday having horses, Diana and I had moved the family into a rambling, ranch-style house on the outskirts of Phoenix, in an area zoned for horses. Our little acre-and-a-half would someday make a nice place to keep two or three horses, but that day had not yet come. Raising three children and trying to give them the best education we could left little money for buying horses, to say nothing of a truck, trailer, saddles, tack, fencing, barn, feed, and veterinary bills.

Partners

Fortunately, Thunder came into my life about that time. Thunder was a twelve-year-old, registered American Paint Horse gelding, a beautiful sorrel and white tobiano. He belonged to Phyllis Bechtel, the mother of Diana's talent agent, Ruth Leighton. Phyllis loved that horse dearly and had raised him from a foal, doting on him like one of her children. Thunder had received top-notch

> A healthy, well-trained horse in the prime of his life, Thunder needed to be ridden.

training and had been shown in both English and Western classes. But Phyllis couldn't ride anymore and that meant Thunder spent most of his time standing in a box stall at one boarding facility or another. A healthy, well-trained horse in the prime of his life, Thunder needed to be ridden.

Phyllis and I met and hit it off immediately. She knew I was serious about doing right by Thunder, and gave me *carte blanche* to ride him as often as I wanted. Over the next few years, I did just that, exploring the undeveloped desert north of Phoenix countless times on Thunder's back. Usually I rode by myself. I told no one where I was going and the truth was, I never knew where I was going. Thunder and I just headed out into the desert. I had no cell phone and the only headgear I wore was a rumpled straw cowboy hat. It was with Thunder that I had my first sense of connection with a horse.

It was with Thunder that I had my closest brush with death.

It was also with Thunder that I had my closest brush with death.

Too Close for Comfort

It happened one Saturday morning in the summer of 1996 on a trail ride with my buddy, Al Raitano. Al is an icon, a singer and entertainer from the old school, the school where you wear a tuxedo when you perform and work so hard to show people a good time that your tuxedo is dripping wet at the end of the evening. I had hired him to mimic Frank Sinatra on a jingle for Peter Piper Pizza and that's when we discovered we shared a passion for horses as well as music.

Al was on his favorite horse, a black nineteen-year-old Arab named Dark Flame, or Darkie, and I was on Thunder. We had a wonderful, laugh-filled ride, and caught up on what each of us had been doing. About 9:00 A.M., it was getting warm and time to head back to the barn. We came to the narrow highway that separated Thunder's boarding facility from open desert, and casually waited for traffic to clear.

"Rick," he said in an even voice, "those are firecrackers."

We heard the car before we saw it. Approaching from the west was a 1950-something four-door Chevy sedan full of teenaged boys, music and laughter pouring out the windows. Al and I had been boys once. We knew that just about anything could happen, so we turned our horses toward the car, backed them up a bit, and went on high alert.

As the car rumbled by, the boy riding shotgun yelled something and threw a paper bag at us. It landed under Thunder's feet, and when I didn't hear glass breaking, I was relieved. I figured it was trash, probably hamburger wrappers and cold French fries. Then I saw the smoke.

Al got a better look. "Rick," he said in an even voice, "those are firecrackers."

About the moment that the thought registered in my brain, the string of Black Cats began exploding in a noisy chain reaction.

"Pop, pop … popopop!"

White smoke and bits of paper wafted up from around Thunder's feet. Cars and trucks whizzed by on the highway a few feet away.

Instincts Take Over

Thunder threw his head up and gathered himself to take flight. For some reason, I pulled on the left rein only and, instead of trying to hold him back, I let him move in a tight circle above the firecrackers. He couldn't see the source of the sound and the acrid smell, and that was probably a good thing. I sensed that Al was doing something similar with Darkie, keeping the horse moving and thinking about placement of his feet. If either horse panicked, we could be in trouble.

If either horse panicked, we could be in trouble.

Finally, after eight or ten seconds, the noise ended. The Chevy had long since faded into the distance.

"You okay?" I yelled through the smoke as I tightened the circle and brought Thunder to a stop.

"Yeah. How 'bout you, cowboy?" Al shot back with a grin.

"Never better!" I replied and we both started laughing the kind of nervous laugh you laugh because it's better than crying. We both felt the gravity of what had just happened. Riders have been killed when their horses spooked into traffic. Al and I sat there for a moment, rubbing our horses and letting it all sink in before we crossed the highway and ended our ride.

I had been given a powerful incentive to learn more about what makes horses tick.

I knew I had been lucky. I knew that if Thunder had been less experienced or less levelheaded, if I hadn't supported him in just the right way, if we had been a few steps closer to the highway, if Al's horse had spooked

... if any of a hundred factors had been different, the outcome could have been disastrous.

As it was, I had been given a powerful incentive to learn more about what makes horses tick: my survival could depend upon it.

Today, the open desert where Al and I rode is filled with expensive homes, but that narrow highway looks much the same. And it still carries the same name: Dynamite Road.

Insights

- Riding can become life-threatening in an instant.
- The general public doesn't understand the survival instinct of horses.
- A panicking horse needs to be given something to think about.
- Bending a horse gives the rider more control in an emergency.

TRY THIS

Source of Power

You'll need a friend for this. Stand with your feet shoulder-width apart, planted firmly on the ground, knees flexed slightly. Have your friend attempt to pull you off balance. Notice that you have plenty of power to resist when your feet are parallel. Now cross one leg over the other and repeat the exercise. Notice how easily your partner can pull you off balance and how quickly your mind goes to your feet. It is this principle we use with a horse to bring his mind back to thinking rather than reacting.

3 Radio

Finding a Place in the Horse Industry

All the while I was developing this fire in the belly about horses, I was making my living as the owner and operator of Lambchops Studios, an audio production company in Phoenix. My specialty was commercials.

In 1990, I had married Diana Baines, a lovely actress who worked regularly at Lambchops. Her daughter and my two sons became our three kids. Life was good, but there were still lean times, times when the phone just didn't ring, and in 1994 I set my mind to finding a way to diversify the business. I found it when a client offered me the production responsibilities for a group of live national talk radio programs.

Into the World of Talk Radio

During the next two years, my staff and I worked on fifteen syndicated radio shows, all owned and managed by other people. None was really successful and most were dismal failures. When it became too difficult to get paid for our services, I resigned those accounts. But something good came out of the experience: I learned how syndicated radio programs were supposed to work.

It's a barter system. A producer offers a radio program to a station at no charge. The station airs the show at no charge. The producer keeps some of the commercial slots, or *avails*, to sell to national advertisers and the station keeps some to sell to local advertisers.

The producer of a syndicated program needs to sign lots of radio stations to attract national sponsors and radio stations want to see enough national sponsors involved with the program to ensure that it will be around for a while. Thus, syndicated radio is a classic vicious circle; you need stations to get sponsors and sponsors to get stations.

Syndicated radio is a classic vicious circle: you need stations to get sponsors and sponsors to get stations.

The idea came to me that I was in a unique position. I could produce a syndicated radio show that avoided the usual pitfalls. The cost would be negligible if it was prerecorded in my studio and if I served as host. We could mail the show to stations instead of feeding it to satellite. It wouldn't be a live show with listeners calling in, but if the content were good enough, I reasoned, the calls wouldn't be missed.

It was a solid plan. The only question was what the show would be about. I knew I couldn't sustain any enthusiasm over the usual topics: current events, politics, health, finance, home improvement, car repair, sports, or relationships.

The Horse Show

"Why not do a show about horses?" Diana asked.

"Why not do a show about horses?" Diana asked.

That was it. From that moment, everything seemed to fall in place as though it were meant to be. It was a marriage of the thing that excited me most—horses—and the thing I had the most skill doing—audio production.

The cherry on top was that the horse industry's biggest advertiser, the Farnam Companies, happened to be headquartered in Phoenix and was a regular production client at our studio. I pitched Farnam the idea of being our charter sponsor and they agreed. It was the perfect way to prime the sponsorship pump. Other sponsors followed Farnam's lead and by the time the first episode of *The Horse Show with Rick Lamb* aired on April 19, 1997, I had eight stations carrying it and a positive cash flow. That alone set us apart from most startup radio programs. We were off to a great start.

Producing *The Horse Show* each week proved to be the easy part. Getting sponsors was about what I expected it to be, a matter of sending out lots of proposals and making lots of pitches. The hardest part of the whole syndicated radio thing was, and still is, signing stations to carry the program.

Radio is a survivor. It's the oldest and most resilient of the electronic media. One reason is that it finds ways to reinvent itself to stay relevant to its customers, the listeners. Stations change with the times. Formats come and go. People come and go. And of course, programs come and go. Syndicated programs are usually the first on the chopping block. This is a dual-edged sword. It's good if you're pitching a show to a station because it might open up a slot for you. But it's bad if you're the one getting cut. All things considered, *The Horse Show with Rick Lamb*, which has been on the air for more than a decade, has had a very stable life in syndication.

It seemed that most radio stations had at least one employee who was into horses. If I managed to connect with that person and get him or her excited about the program, we had a good chance of adding the station to our network. Money was always the primary issue. Would local advertisers be interested in buying radio ads in and around this program?

Money wasn't the only consideration, however. Some stations added our show and kept it on the air simply because they liked it. They considered it a service to their listeners.

The Horse Show Minute

There was one objection that I couldn't overcome. For some stations, usually those that played lots of music, the show was just too long. Even though we offered it as a one or two-hour weekend program, some stations couldn't clear that much time in their schedules or didn't want to deviate from the music format that long. Many of these stations felt that a show about horses was a good idea and that their audience would listen. It just needed to be shorter.

After hearing that enough times, I got the message. I needed a second syndicated radio show on horses, one that was as short as possible. In

October of 1999, we launched *The Horse Show Minute*, a weekday radio feature.

Every month, I wrote and recorded at least twenty one-minute programs. Each program consisted of a fifteen-second sound bite from a guest on my long show, with forty-five seconds of my commentary surrounding it. Topics varied widely but every minute program gave the listener something interesting or educational to take away. It was amazing how much could be packed into those sixty-second shows. More important, writing the commentary crystallized my own thinking on the things I was learning about horses.

> **Writing the commentary crystallized my own thinking on the things I was learning.**

As I expected, *The Horse Show Minute* was relatively easy to pitch, and in no time at all, I had created a separate network of radio stations carrying that program. I was on a roll, doing what people with far more experience in radio had not been able to do. At the same time, I was making progress on my journey from human to Horseman.

But there was something eating at me inside.

Insights

- Horse owners and enthusiasts want to learn more about horses.
- Radio is a viable medium for teaching.
- Other people want to know the same things I want to know.
- The American horse industry is huge and ripe with opportunity.

TRY THIS

Provide Your Own Pictures

In this exercise, you'll discover the power of visualization. Turn on your favorite television drama, but don't watch it; listen to it. Notice how much more engaged your mind becomes in the subject matter. Your mind must conjure up images for everything it hears, instead of simply accepting the visuals presented on the screen. This is one reason radio and audio books remain popular.

4 Mr. Curiosity
Channeling the Passion to Learn

People thought I was fearless, diving headlong into national radio the way I did. But that wasn't true. I worried about whether I could do it. Not so much making *The Horse Show* work as a business, and certainly not the audio part—I could do that in my sleep.

My concern was the hosting part.

Banter didn't come naturally to me. As a child, I was so shy around strangers that I wouldn't go to birthday parties. I didn't like to play games because I didn't want to be the center of attention, even for a moment.

I'd played music professionally since I was fourteen, but I was never the front man, the guy who talked to the audience.

Once, when I was in my twenties, I was a guest in the home of entertainer Peter Marshall. His son,

It's hard to imagine anyone less suited to talk radio.

Pete, and I were friends. Mr. Marshall picked up immediately on my shyness and started calling me "the Talker." I wanted so badly to be chatty but the words wouldn't come.

Reinvention

Now in my forties, things hadn't changed all that much. Inside, I was still a shy person. It's hard to imagine anyone less suited to talk radio. Still I knew I could learn. I had reinvented myself before and I could do it again. But would people want to listen to my guests and me in the meantime?

The question that haunted me the most, however, was how I would feel about horses in the future. I was as horse crazy as a twelve-year-old girl, but would it last? What if I woke up one day and no longer cared?

That day never came. In fact, I became crazier about horses as the years went by. As for my insecurity about hosting, I discovered that honesty and enthusiasm go a long way. I didn't need the deepest voice, the funniest banter, or the most profound analysis. I didn't have to be the best radio host ever; I just had to be the best Rick Lamb I could be. That's all my audience really wanted from me.

The Gift of Curiosity

I did realize along the way that I had something important going for me. I am naturally curious.

The English author, critic, and lexicographer, Samuel Johnson (1709–1784), left us a famous quote about curiosity: "Curiosity is one of the permanent and certain characteristics of a vigorous mind." It's good in horses, too. Pat Parelli once told me that curiosity is the opposite of fear in a horse. If a horse displays curiosity, you know he's ready to learn.

> "Curiosity is one of the permanent and certain characteristics of a vigorous mind."

When it comes to curiosity, I think you either have it or you don't. I'm curious about horses, but I'm also curious about almost everything around me. How does that work? Who made that? How would it feel to have that job? What was she like as a child? What was he trying to say with that painting? Questions run through my head all the time. On my radio show, I just give them voice. The biggest question of all, of course, is *why*. Why did you make that choice? Why do you feel that way? And so on.

Curiosity generates enthusiasm and that appeals to listeners.

Guests Welcome

From the beginning, horse people of all stripes were willing to be guests on my radio show, especially if they had something they wanted to promote—a book, a video, a stallion, an event. All I had to do was ask. As more people became familiar with my name, it got even easier. After all, being a guest on my show was free national exposure. At first the shows were heard on radio only. Then I added streaming, so people could listen online. A subscription CD came next, and finally podcasts. Anyone anywhere could listen to my shows anytime they wanted.

> Free publicity wasn't the only reason people liked being on my show.

But free publicity wasn't the only reason people liked being on my show. I took great care in how I treated my guests. Because the show was not live, I had the opportunity to edit what they said. I always told nervous guests, "Don't worry. I'll make us both sound brilliant."

This was a responsibility I took seriously. My audience deserved quality information and entertainment. There wasn't much value in listening to me or a guest stammering around, looking for the right way to say something. On the other hand, I was careful to never change the meaning of what was said or make an interview sound like it was edited.

The time I spent editing interviews also helped me on my journey. It gave me repeated exposure to what each of my guests said about horses, the way they think and the ways we can train and care for them, allowing me to retain a whole lot more of it.

The Art of the Interview

Speaking of interviews, people tell me all the time that I'm a great interviewer. It's very flattering to hear. In fact, the highest compliment a listener can give me is to say, "You ask the questions *I* want to ask." My job is to represent the listener, to ask the obvious question, and the probing question, and the question that will cause the final piece of the puzzle to fall in place.

> My job is to ask both the obvious question and the probing question.

A good radio host is a professional conversationalist, a person skilled at the give and take of conversation. There is a certain rhythm to a good conversation. I have to create and maintain that rhythm. But sometimes guests ramble on and on, or stumble over their words and get rattled. That's when I have to jump in, summarize, finish a point, or steer the conversation another way without embarrassing the guest. It's like I'm a rescue swimmer in a sea of words. If I do it well, no one even notices.

Radio gave me the opportunity to be right in the middle of the horse industry. Principles and training methods started coming at me from all directions, and as I organized and passed them on to my listeners, I learned.

My journey picked up its pace and I was very pleased with myself.

Insights

- Curiosity, in humans and horses, is a good thing.
- People can reinvent themselves if they are willing to work at it.
- How well you listen is as important as how well you speak.

TRY THIS

Become a Better Listener

To become a more effective listener, make it an active mental process rather than a passive physiological process. As you listen, try to predict what the speaker is about to say and then see if you're right. Whether you are right or not doesn't matter. You're still actively involved in the subject matter being discussed. By the way, your brain operates at a much faster rate than anyone can speak, so you are perfectly capable of listening and thinking about what is being said at the same time.

5 A Perfect Morning
Overconfidence Rears Its Ugly Head

Life has a way of taking you down a notch or two when you get to thinking you're something special. With me it happened about two years into my journey, early one September morning in 1998.

I had arrived at sunrise to get in a quick ride on Thunder before heading to the studio to work on my radio show. Usually when I rode early, Thunder had already been fed by the hired help at the barn. This day there was still some hay left in his feeder when I haltered him and led him to the saddling area.

The Agenda

A short distance from the barn lay an oval riding track, inside of which were a couple acres of natural desert that doubled as a turnout area. When Thunder and I walked out onto the track, I was happy to find it empty and recently groomed. The dirt and sand mix that made up the footing looked neat and clean, the tine grooves still visible. Riding on that track was like skiing on fresh powder. I took a deep breath of the clean morning air, adjusted my reins, and gave Thunder a gentle squeeze with my legs. He moved into an easy trot.

Riding on that track was like skiing on fresh powder.

We made a full lap on the track counterclockwise, then did the same thing clockwise. All went well. My posting was getting smoother. I wanted to be so good at posting that it looked effortless. So many riders post in such an exaggerated way that it makes me tired just watching them. I knew it could be better than that.

When I completed the second lap I leaned forward, moved my rein hand forward on Thunder's neck, made a kissing sound, and squeezed again with my calves. It was time to canter. In fact, my plan was to do quite a bit of cantering that morning, several laps around the track in each direction. It would be good for Thunder, who still didn't get as much exercise as he needed, and good for me. There could be no better way to start the day, I thought.

Thunder reluctantly picked up a rough canter. It felt different than usual. I tried to adjust to it but couldn't really get into the rhythm. Maybe he was simply on the wrong lead for going around that oval track. Maybe he was cross-cantering—cantering on one lead with his front legs and the opposite lead with his hind legs. I did feel certain, though, that whatever he was doing, he was doing by choice. Like any horse, Thunder could be lazy at times and that morning he was probably also irritable about being dragged away from his breakfast to go round and round on this silly track.

A Bad Decision

"Well, now," I thought to myself, "we'll see who's leader of this team."

With the end of my reins, I gave Thunder a sharp slap on the right hip. In all the hours we'd spent together, I'd never done that before. Worse, I gave him no warning that it was coming. I didn't escalate the pressure of my cue gradually; I jumped from simply suggesting a canter to spanking him hard. I skipped several steps in my use of pressure. It was like telling a child quietly, "No," and then whacking him roughly on the rear end.

It was like telling a child quietly, "No," then whacking him roughly on the rear end.

Looking back, I had the right idea but the wrong execution. Thunder was perfectly capable of giving me a nice coordinated canter that morning. Instead he chose to test me. "Will you let me get away with this pathetic performance?" was the question in his mind.

If it happened to me today, I might stop Thunder immediately and back him up energetically for 10 or 20 yards. Backing takes more effort than going forward for a horse and it's not something he normally does in nature. Backing is a submissive act that reinforces the rider as the dominant member of the team and helps with many equine attitude issues.

> If it happened to me today, I might stop Thunder immediately and back him up for 10 or 20 yards.

I might also drop him back to a trot, and then ask him very clearly to take the right lead when he stepped into the canter. We were going clockwise on the track at the time this happened, so the right lead was the correct lead.

I might also do exactly what I did—turn up the heat and let him sort out the best way to carry himself—but I would do it a little bit at a time. I would start by spanking my own thighs lightly with the reins in an over-and-under motion. Thunder would feel the increase in my energy and see it with his peripheral vision. He would know I wanted more of a try from him. If that didn't work, if he didn't give me a noticeable increase in effort, I would then do the same on his flanks on both sides. The reins slapping lightly on his flanks wouldn't hurt him, but it would be annoying and he would know absolutely that I expected him to pick up his speed. If this, too, failed to produce a result, I would then be perfectly justified in spanking him hard with the reins, again on one side and then the other, to get him to speed up. He would find that going faster in such a discombobulated way was more work than getting on the correct lead and settling into an even canter.

There are several things I could have done that would have worked better than what I did. At the time I had enough knowledge to recognize that

CONTROLLING LEADS

When a horse is cantering on a right lead, for instance, he is reaching forward a bit farther with his right hind leg and right front leg than his left hind and front. His entire body is carried in such a way that he can bend or turn to the right easily. To ask for a right lead, the rider tips the horse's nose a little to the right and presses behind the girth with his left heel or leg. When a horse is very in tune with a rider, merely shifting weight in the saddle is enough to cue the horse to take the desired lead. Changing leads while cantering is known as a *flying lead change*.

Thunder was testing me, but not enough experience to know how to handle it. What happened next left me with plenty to think about for years to come.

Insights

- Backing up cures many attitude problems with horses.
- Pressure applied should start at low levels and increase in measured steps.
- Confidence is good; overconfidence is dangerous.

TRY THIS

Carry Yourself with a Confident Bearing

Overconfidence can get you in trouble with a horse, but lack of confidence is equally dangerous, as it tells a horse he needs to take over leadership of the team.

Practice approaching your horse with your head up, eyes clear and focused, pace unhurried but deliberate, as though you've done this a thousand times before. Avoid quick, jerky movements around your horse and keep your breathing even. These are all signs of confidence. Even if you don't feel confident, acting confident will help.

6 **The Fall**
Getting Hurt Changes Everything

My first mistake on that perfect September morning was spanking Thunder hard. It was a cue I had not used with him before and it came out of nowhere, with too much intensity behind it. My second mistake was not having a deep seat at the time I did it. I wasn't melted into the saddle, weight low and centered, with my shoulders back and my feet secure in the stirrups. In fact, my weight was more forward; I might have been looking down at his front legs as I spanked him.

> **I slid headfirst off Thunder's right shoulder.**

Back on the Ground

Thunder did not buck. It was more of a little kick out with both hind legs. Still, it was enough to unseat me, and I slid headfirst off his right shoulder.

It felt like slow motion and I had plenty of time to make a plan before I hit the ground. Unfortunately, I didn't. I'd never thought about what I should do in such a situation. It never occurred to me to tuck and roll as I hit the ground. All I can remember thinking as I fell those few feet from the saddle to the ground is wanting to get there as quickly as I could.

Instinctively, I reached down with both arms, which caused me to flip in midair and land flat on my back, like a TV wrestler being smacked down. Wrestlers bounce a bit when they hit the canvas. I didn't.

The freshly tilled footing of the track softened the impact, but I still knew immediately that I was hurt. I couldn't move and had trouble breathing. For what seemed like several minutes, I simply lay there sucking in as much air as I could and trying to not panic. A mature mesquite tree stood between the barn and me so no one could see my plight. It saved me some embarrassment but also ruled out any immediate help. For a while, at least, I was on my own.

When my breathing returned to normal, I gritted my teeth, rolled onto my right side, and pushed myself carefully to a sitting position. My lower back felt heavy and tight, but it didn't seem like anything was broken.

I wasn't sure I could stand, but I knew I had to try. I also knew that it was going to hurt. I cleared my mind and let the adrenaline already coursing through my body do its job. Slowly I made my way first to my knees, then to my feet. I was standing, but I was hunched over like a man twice my age, huffing as though I'd just run a mile.

Looking down the track, I saw Thunder standing quietly and watching me from a few yards away, reins hanging to the ground. "Oh, that's good," I thought. "Someone has taught him to ground tie." It's funny what goes through your head at times like that. I inched my way toward him and took up the reins. For a brief, crazy moment, I considered climbing back on, but common sense prevailed, and, setting my sights on the barn, I began one of the longest walks of my life.

> For a brief, crazy moment, I considered climbing back on.

The Long Way Home

With each step back to the barn, pain reverberated through my body. I forced myself to focus, and what emerged from the thoughts swirling around in my brain were two words: *never again*. I repeated them over and over like a mantra. No matter what, this must never, ever happen again.

At the barn, I took the saddle, pad, bridle, and protective boots off Thunder and put them in the tack room. He was exceptionally calm as I put him in his stall. I think he knew something bad had happened. I secured the stall door and went straight to my truck.

Somehow I managed to get home. By the end of the twenty-minute drive, I was leaning over the steering wheel, my chest nearly touching it, my swollen back forcing me to the edge of the seat.

"Diana, I need your help," I called out as I hobbled through the side door of the house. When I saw her, tears filled my eyes. She pulled up my T-shirt and took a look, letting out a small gasp in spite of herself. My lower back looked as though someone had cut a volleyball in half and put it under my skin.

I wasn't worried about ever riding again.

"Rick, we're going straight to the emergency room," she said, trying to sound calm.

The doctor on duty ordered X-rays and as I lay on that cold table waiting, I wondered for the first time what the future would hold for me. I wasn't worried about ever riding again. I was worried about walking normally again.

The X-rays showed extensive soft tissue trauma but no broken bones. I was lucky, everyone told me.

For several days, I lay in bed, my lower back packed with ice. I was on crutches for two weeks and sore for several months. For many years after, I had a noticeable bump over my tailbone and felt discomfort whenever I lay on my back to exercise.

Residual Fear

It was probably a year before I forced myself to go ride Thunder again. By then Phyllis had moved him to another barn, one without such easy access to the desert. That became a convenient excuse for not riding, and my visits to Thunder became fewer and fewer.

I still loved horses but I was fighting down another emotion: fear.

I was in a quandary. I was gaining a following on radio and people were beginning to think of me as an authority on horses. I still loved horses but I was fighting down another emotion: fear.

Still, I didn't give up on becoming a Horseman. My journey had taken an unexpected detour but I was determined to keep it moving forward and I felt certain that the way to do that was to get a horse of my own.

Insights

- Be certain to have a secure seat before giving any sort of cue to a horse.

- Everyone becomes less resilient with age.

- A second's worth of bad judgment can produce years of suffering.

TRY THIS

Emergency Dismount

It is usually better to stay on a horse that is bucking or bolting, rather than try to get off in the heat of the moment. However, if you feel *absolutely certain* that you are going to come off the horse, it is better to get off on your own terms. That is the purpose of the emergency dismount.

- The first step is to get your feet out of the stirrups and to be certain you are not entangled in the reins. You must avoid being dragged at all costs.

- The second step is to lean forward, push off the horse's neck (or the saddle horn, if you are riding in a Western saddle) and throw your legs out behind you. This will get you off the horse's back and headed toward the ground.

- The third step is to collapse, tuck, and roll when you hit the ground. Staying loose will minimize injury. Do not try to hold onto the reins during all of this. Your safety is more important than keeping control of the horse.

Finally, it is best to practice this maneuver ahead of time in a controlled setting with a dependable horse. Try it at the walk first, then the trot. Having a plan will help immensely should an emergency dismount become necessary.

7 Lambs and Horses
Taking the Plunge into Horse Ownership

"I feel like a ten-year-old going to Disneyland!" Diana said as we pulled out of our driveway in Phoenix that hot July morning in 2001.

"Me, too!" I replied with a laugh. The trip we had planned for so long was finally underway. We were headed for the tall pines and cool, mountain meadows of Pagosa Springs, Colorado. Our destination was one of the horse meccas of the West, the Parelli International Study Center, a 400-acre horse ranch that served as Pat and Linda Parelli's home and as center of their growing education empire. The purpose of our trip was to select two horses of our own, the result of a trade I had done with Pat for some national radio advertising. I had a secret agenda with these horses: to lose my fear of riding.

At the time, Pat had an affiliation with another ranch—La Cense Montana—that specialized in raising foundation-bred Quarter Horses in a natural setting, giving them some basic Parelli training, then selling them. Each year, the best of these horses were sent to a sister ranch near Paris, France, where they brought top dollar from Europeans wanting good-looking "cowboy horses" with the Parelli stamp of approval. The group of horses from which we would pick was on its way to Europe with a brief layover in Colorado. Thus, they were the cream of the La Cense Montana crop that year.

Horse Shopping

When we arrived at the ranch, we found Linda busy teaching a Level 2 class in Parelli Natural Horsemanship. We watched for a bit and marveled again at what a great teacher and hard worker she is. Pat greeted us warmly, gave us a list of the horses available, and drove us straight to the pen in his golf cart. There were fifteen to twenty horses milling about. We watched as one of his advanced students stirred up the herd and got them interacting with one another.

A seasoned horse trader would have seen those horses much differently than we did.

A seasoned horse trader would have seen those horses much differently than we did. With nothing else to go on, and confident they were all good, solid horses, we made our choices based on looks.

How different I would do it today! Any horse that was a serious contender would spend time with me on groundwork—not to see what he already knew, but how he felt about my being leader and how willing he was to move his feet—and then we would take a nice long ride, both with and without other horses. I would see how he reacted to being tied, how he felt about being handled all over, and particularly how he accepted my handling his feet.

Diana selected Coins, a sturdy five-year-old gelding. Sorrel with a white blaze and four white socks, he looked like he was made to work cattle with a cowboy on his back. I selected a similar gelding named Champion.

A pre-purchase exam is a must for any horse at any price.

We booked a local veterinarian to perform pre-purchase exams the next morning. I learned early in my journey that a pre-purchase exam is a must before assuming responsibility for any horse at any price. It cannot predict the future, but it can uncover some medical issues that may affect the suitability of a horse for a given purpose.

Coins received a clean bill of health in all departments, but Champion had some minor lameness issues the vet uncovered in her exam. I went back to the pen to find another horse.

Most experts recommend geldings for first-time horse owners, so on the previous day, I had not paid any attention to the mares. This time, one of them caught my eye. A coppery sorrel color, with a Hollywood-perfect blazed face and two white socks on the rear, she was a bit smaller than most of the other horses, and she was barefoot. In fact, there was no sign she had ever been shod, which appealed to me. This mare was gorgeous and feminine, but it was the look in her eye that stopped me cold. It was depth or sweetness or intelligence, or perhaps all three. Whatever it was, I knew I'd found my horse.

> This mare was gorgeous and feminine, but it was the look in her eye that stopped me cold.

I looked up her hip number on the log sheet and found that her name was Candidas Sun—or Candy—and that she was priced a bit higher than most of the other horses. I found that odd because she had obviously sustained an injury to her right hind cannon bone at some point in the past. A jagged scar remained and the area was slightly enlarged. It did not affect her movement and she vetted just fine.

That injury actually proved to be a blessing. Candy was a great-grand-daughter of the World Champion cutting horse, Cutter Bill, so she had good breeding to go along with her good looks. Without that scar, she would have been a prime prospect for a show career and would have been priced much higher, right out of my price range. For my purposes, however, she was just fine. Actually, she was more than fine. She was perfect.

> Pat asked if we would consider leaving the horses there for the rest of the summer.

While we were handling the paperwork in the ranch office, Pat asked if we would consider leaving the horses there for the rest of the summer. They would get additional training at the hands of some of his advanced students, who needed more horses to work with. He also pointed out that it would be easier on the horses to acclimate to the Phoenix heat slowly rather than being dropped into it in the middle of summer. We agreed and made plans to return on September 15, 2001.

Terror Hits Home

On September 11, 2001, radical Islamic terrorists took control of four commercial airliners, crashed two of them into the World Trade Center towers in New York City and a third into the Pentagon outside Washing-

ton, D.C. The fourth hijacked plane went down in rural Pennsylvania after heroic passengers stormed the cockpit to reclaim control. This attack

**Were there more terrorists
in our midst?**

on America, within our borders, profoundly affected
all of us. It was the single most disturbing, memorable, and significant event in the fifty years I had been
on the planet. More than 3,000 innocent Americans
died that day. Most of them were just regular folks like Diana and me.

In the days that immediately followed 9/11, fear and uncertainty per-
vaded every aspect of American life. Were there more terrorists in our
midst? Would there be more attacks? Should we avoid air travel? Were all
Muslims now our enemies? There were far more questions than answers.
Clearly, America had entered a new era.

By September 14, there were little signs that life might return to some
kind of normalcy for those of us not directly affected by the attacks. Diana and I decided to go ahead with our trip to get the horses.

When we arrived at the ranch, the mood was somber. We were invited to stay for dinner that evening and did so, eating in the dining hall
with Pat, Linda, family, friends, and students. It felt good to be with fellow horse lovers at a time like that. Pat also invited us to get a bit of
instruction in handling our horses before we took them home the next
day. Wanting to get an early start, we at first declined, but Pat pressed.
I'm glad he did.

The following morning, we received some one-on-one instruction in
the Seven Games, a series of groundwork exercises that form an integral
part of the Parelli approach. Karen Scholl, who had resigned her job as
president of Parelli Natural Horsemanship to become an instructor in
the method, helped us immensely that day. We probably knew Karen
better than anyone else in the organization and years later, when she had
moved on to develop her own training and teaching system, she would
become a dear friend and invaluable help with our horses.

The Trailering

On that day, after we had worked and played with Coins and Candy for
the better part of two hours, the weather turned ugly. With eleven hours

of driving ahead of us, Diana and I decided it was time to hit the road. The sky darkened and snowflakes began to fall as Karen taught our horses to go into our trailer. You couldn't have picked worse conditions under which to teach that important lesson but Karen did a fine job. We secured all the doors and left the ranch amid snow flurries with me at the wheel, both knowing that Diana would end up doing the bulk of the driving while I dozed in the passenger seat.

The snow turned to blinding rain with thunder and lightening as we headed toward Phoenix.

The snow turned to blinding rain with thunder and lightening as we headed out of the mountains toward Phoenix. Never having pulled horses in a trailer, we had a few tense moments in that storm and worried how our new horses were faring.

It was late at night when we got home. Unloading the horses for the first time in a strange place after a long, difficult ride would be challenging enough. Doing it at night with the limited experience I had at the time made it that much harder.

I untied the lead ropes and released the butt bar on Coins' side first. Coins blasted out of the trailer, nearly knocking me down and ripping the lead rope through my hands. I caught the end of

Coins blasted out of the trailer, nearly knocking me down and ripping the lead rope through my hands.

it and finally got him under control. He was a mess, his tail matted and covered with manure, broken hairs sticking out every direction. He had obviously pushed against the butt bar the whole trip, instead of standing squarely in the trailer.

Candy was calmer but I did notice that she had broken the latch on the escape door, apparently after getting her halter caught on it. Candy would get over any bad memories she had of that first trip and become an easy traveler.

Coins wouldn't.

Insights

- First-time horse owners should never buy a horse based on looks alone.

- A pre-purchase exam is necessary to identify medical issues that may affect a horse's suitability for the buyer's purposes.

- Groundwork is important to learn for both the horse and the handler.

- A horse should be introduced to trailering gradually, with trips getting progressively longer.

TRY THIS

Set Up for Trailer Loading Success

There are numerous effective methods for teaching a horse to calmly enter and exit a trailer. Regardless of the method you use, these suggestions will make it go more smoothly:

- Set aside an entire day for the first lesson and leave your wristwatch at home.

- Teach the lesson in a large confined area, such as an arena or pasture.

- Leave the trailer attached to the truck for maximum stability.

- Once the horse is in the trailer, ask him to back out before he does so on his own.

- Repeat the lesson until the horse will stay in the trailer without being restrained.

8 The Trouble with Coins
A Classic Mismatch of Horse and Human

Coins was to be Diana's horse, but she became uncomfortable with him early on and never did ride him. He was the alpha horse and at times, he would go after Candy aggressively. There was nothing I could do to stop it, and I was committed to letting them work it out between themselves, anyway. It amazed me to see how quickly these incidents passed. Moments later, the two would be standing side by side eating hay as if they were the best of friends. Candy did not seem to be afraid of Coins.

The Phobia

Coins was never aggressive toward me, but he still posed a threat because he had a phobia about being tied. Maybe it came from the difficult trailer ride home from the Parelli Ranch. Maybe it was there all along. Maybe in Coins, the natural feelings of claustrophobia that all horses experience from time to time were particularly strong.

> A horse's number one means of survival is running away— and when he can't do that, panic may ensue.

It's easy to understand how horses could develop a fear of confinement. A horse's number one means of survival is running away. When he can't do that because he's tied or confined in a trailer, panic may ensue.

Coins would accept tying for a while, but any little thing could cause him to panic and pull back until something broke. His blasting out of the trailer the first time I unloaded him was symptomatic of that problem.

Horses need to unload slowly and under the control of the handler. In fact, it's just as important to teach a horse to unload calmly upon command, as it is to teach him to load calmly upon command.

Loose in the Desert

In one of my attempts to work with Coins, I took him to Horse Lovers' Park, an equestrian preserve near our home, to ride him in one of its arenas. The ride didn't go particularly well and he certainly didn't work up a sweat, but afterward, I thought I would hose him off anyway. I led him to one of several public wash racks and tied him to the front of the rack. He didn't seem to mind, so I began to spray him down. As soon as he felt the water, he pulled back hard, breaking the snap on the lead rope, and trotting off toward the open desert. I tried hard not to panic. There was nothing stopping Coins from disappearing into the hundreds of acres of mesquite trees, scrub brush, and cactus that comprised the preserve, or from wandering back to Tatum Road, the busy street at its entrance.

> **Coins pulled back hard, breaking the snap on the lead rope.**

I knew I had to catch him and I remembered what I had heard several guests say on my radio show: if you act like you're trying to catch the horse, he will be much harder to catch. If he's in an arena or even a pasture, you can be very nonchalant about the whole thing because you know he can't get away. But Coins wasn't contained in any way. Every human instinct told me to run after him and throw my arms around him, to apply muscle and speed to the problem. Fortunately, my brain remained in control.

> **Every human instinct told me to apply muscle and speed to the problem.**

Someone had given me some horse cookies and they were still in the trailer. I casually walked back, stuffed the cookies in my shirt pocket, and looked for our other lead rope. It wasn't there. I had left it at home, hanging on a hook in the breezeway.

Coins had stopped trotting and was foraging around among some bushes, 50 yards or so from the wash rack. I walked in his general direction, but made certain I didn't look directly at him. Instead, I looked at the lead rope with the broken snap in my hands. I would have to tie the rope onto his halter if and when I caught him. At least I still remembered my knots from Boy Scouts. It would take a few seconds, though. He would have to stand there quietly in the meantime. I hoped he would do that.

Reverse Psychology

I continued on a meandering, zigzagging course toward Coins. He ignored me and continued eating. Finally, I was only a couple feet away. My gut told me to throw the rope over his head and physically restrain him. Again, I remembered what I had been taught and resisted the impulse. I stood there quietly for a few moments, not looking directly at him, acting preoccupied with something else. Finally I reached out and rubbed him on the withers, then the neck, using long, gentle strokes. Again, I stopped and turned away.

Finally, curiosity got the best of Coins and he raised his head to investigate.

Coins continued grazing. I removed a cookie from my pocket and held it out where I was certain he could see it with his peripheral vision. He ignored me, so I waited. And waited. Finally, curiosity got the best of Coins and he raised his head to investigate. Then he took the cookie from my hand. I gave him a nice rub and stepped back. It felt very unnatural to do that, but I wanted him to come to me now and this sort of reverse psychology was exactly the way to make it happen.

He took another step and received another cookie. As he was munching, I realized that the time was right and I casually tied the lead rope to his halter. I let him stand there a few more minutes and have the last cookie. Then I turned away and began walking toward the trailer. Coins followed willingly. The lead rope drooped between us. There was no need for me to pull him. The outing ended on a positive note, with no further excitement. It had been an important day on my journey.

Health Hazards

The next pulling back episode occurred after I tied Coins in the wash rack of my barn. It was over in less than three seconds. He pulled back, stretching the nylon/poly lead rope to its maximum length. Again, the brass snap broke. As if fired by a giant slingshot, the snap shot back to the barn, missing my head by inches and putting a hole the size of a quarter in the wooden siding. All I could think of was how that hole could have been in my head, or Diana's head or anybody's head. Not long after that, a similar incident occurred in the trailer and again, equipment was damaged.

> The broken snap shot back to the barn, missing my head by inches.

The final straw, however, happened not with Coins tied, but with me holding him while his feet were being trimmed. For a while he stood quietly, then for reasons only he knew, he began throwing his head, making it difficult to do the hoof work. I slipped my right hand inside his rope halter to scratch his face, hoping it would calm him. For a moment it did, then he threw his head violently, wrenching the little finger on my right hand. That finger has been crooked ever since. It was my mistake to allow my hand to become entangled in the halter and every time I look at that crooked little finger, I think of the lesson I learned.

There was nothing wrong with Coins. We were simply the wrong owners for him. He was still young and needed guidance from a better trainer than I. We put Coins up for sale and a Parelli student in Nevada bought him. I was completely honest about the problems we had with him. Today, I'm certain that I could work through all of his issues and have a perfect gentleman for Diana to ride. But not then. Many a fine horseman has lamented to me the horses he couldn't help on his journey for the simple reason that he was not ready. That's exactly how I feel about Coins. I miss him and wonder what might have been.

> There was nothing wrong with Coins. We were simply the wrong owners for him.

Insights

- Fear of confinement is a natural part of the makeup of every horse.
- Some horses panic more easily when tied than others.
- A horse is easier to catch if you do not act like you're trying to catch him.
- It is best to get rid of a horse that is not appropriate for your level of experience.

TRY THIS

Tie with Slippage

If your horse is prone to panicking when tied, you can help him overcome this feeling. You'll do it by tying him in such a way that he can pull some slack if he starts feeling claustrophobic. Teach this in an arena, stall, or other confined area in case he gets away from you.

Start by simply wrapping his lead rope around a corral rail. Use one wrap around at first, so it's easy to pull some slack. When he pulls back, the rope will slip and he'll realized he's not trapped. Once he's done this a few times, he'll become convinced that he's not really tied, after all, and he'll lose interest in getting free. As he becomes more tolerant of being tied, you can add another wrap to make it more difficult. When he will stand tied quietly for at least an hour, without pulling back, you can tie him more solidly. From then on, give your horse plenty of practice standing tied. It is not cruel to the horse; in fact, most will become so comfortable with standing tied that they will use the opportunity to sleep.

Incidentally, the Blocker Tie Ring™ is a simple and highly effective tool for teaching this lesson to the horse and for everyday tying. It offers three degrees of controlled slippage and comes with detailed instructions on teaching a horse to stand tied. I carry this innovative tool with me at all times and try to never tie my horse without it.

9 The Cattle Drive
The Importance of Having a Job to Do

"John, Diana. Diana, John."

I made short work of the introductions, eager to get to the heart of our meeting. Diana and I were in Louisville, Kentucky, at Equitana USA, one of the biggest horse expos in the country in 2001. We were talking to John Flynn, attorney, rancher, novelist, and partner in the Montana High Country Cattle Drive, an authentic working cattle drive in the

Diana and I were enthralled with the idea of a working cattle drive.

Big Belt Mountains of Montana. Although we weren't exactly city slickers, Diana and I were still enthralled with the idea of a working cattle drive, and we had hatched a plan. I began my pitch.

The Deal

"Here's what we can do, John. First, we'll get you on the radio in an interview to talk about your cattle drives and announce that we are going on one of them. Second, we'll run a radio spot campaign where I'll personally invite listeners to come with us. Third, I'll record an audio diary on the drive and make another radio program from that, which would plug your cattle drives for the following year."

John was listening carefully, but his expression was neutral.

"Now, what we would want from you is two places on the first cattle drive of next summer, plus airfare to get the two of us to Montana and back home. This can't cost us anything out of pocket." It was a good deal for John and for us, a classic win-win situation.

John didn't speak for a few moments. The expo ambiance—the chatter of shoppers, the occasional amplified announcement, the whinny of horses heading to arenas or stalls—seemed to rise in volume to fill the void.

"I have to run it by my partners," John finally replied, "but I think we'll probably do it." With that he broke into a smile. I liked this tall, soft-spoken guy and he would impress me more as I got to know him.

"Great!" I said, and reminded myself that now was the time to stop selling and get out of there. "I'll give you a call next week," I promised. We said our goodbyes and Diana and I drifted back into the expo crowd.

Promotion

The partners agreed to our proposal and we set a timetable. I recorded the radio spot and not long after it began airing on my show, I got a call from James Towle, president of Rio Vista Products, a longtime sponsor.

"I like this cattle drive idea," he said. "And we'd like to have a contest to give away a couple trips." It was a photo and essay contest. Send a picture of your horse at his prettiest and tell why you use Rio Vista's grooming products. I liked the idea. John Flynn was thrilled, and we got another radio spot going for the contest.

The cattle drive campaign worked beautifully for everyone. Several guests on that drive were listeners of mine from various parts of the country. The winner of the contest was a young girl named Cassie. Her grandmother accompanied her on the trip.

The cattle drive took place in June 2002, about three-and-a-half years after my fall off Thunder. Although at the time of the ride Diana and I had horses of our own, Coins and Candy, I had ridden very little since the fall, always finding some excuse or another. I had focused what time I spent with the horses on groundwork. Yet here I was going off on a five-day ride on a horse about which I knew nothing, doing work I'd never done before, with listeners watching my every move. I knew it was risky, but I also knew it could be a lot of fun. It was time for me to cowboy up and ride again.

The cattle drive was to start the day after my appearance at the Western States Horse Expo in Sacramento. Unfortunately, plane problems caused us to miss both the orientation and get-acquainted party. By the time we got there, everybody knew one another, but we soon became part of the group. I met several of my listeners and did my best to make them feel comfortable with me.

Working Horses

Diana was assigned a mature mare named Vicky that was a pretty solid citizen. Calm and even a bit lazy by nature, Vicky's only bad habit was going too fast when she became worried about being away from the other horses. If I was nearby, I would get right in front of Diana and Vicky on my horse and slow down the pace. That worked pretty well.

> I would get right in front of Diana and Vicky on my horse and slow down the pace.

Vicky was typical of many horses. Being herd animals, horses are most comfortable when they are around others of their kind. Conversely, they get nervous about being apart. That takes their minds off their riders and onto getting back to the herd. Diana and I managed the problem, but we were only treating the symptoms. The underlying cause—that Vicky didn't really believe she was as safe with Diana as with the other horses—was never addressed.

The horse I was provided for the cattle drive was a red roan Appaloosa gelding. I never heard his age, but he was an experienced horse, for sure. We got along just fine on the first day. I discovered that he had a smooth "single-foot" gait, akin to a very fast walk, that he preferred over a trot. That made him comfortable to ride for the long hours I was in the saddle. He also seemed to have no desire at all to canter, which was just fine with me.

The second day I had a little disagreement with my horse. It happened early in the morning when we began moving cattle up a winding mountain path. He started pulling against the bridle and throwing his head around.

> The second day I had a little disagreement with my horse.

He was unhappy about something or unsure about me. Remembering the firecracker incident and what I was learning from the horsemen I had

43

interviewed, I pulled his head to one side and held him in a tight circle until he settled down. That's all it took to convince him that I could control his movement. We had no further problems, and there were many times during the next few days that I felt he and I were really working as a team.

The cattle drive was wonderful for Diana and me. We realized how much your riding improves when you have a job to do. You get out of your own way. Children are often good riders because they don't overthink it. As adults, we analyze and worry about every little thing. We try to remember and apply everything we've heard anyone say. Heels down, eyes up, back straight, pelvis forward, hands out in front of you. No wonder we tense up when riding. When you do a job on horseback, your conscious mind gets out of the way and you find that the rider inside is not so bad after all.

For me, the cattle drive was a key leg on my journey. It restored my confidence that I could ride a horse, that the joy was still there, that I could be safe, and that the fantasy of having a relationship with a horse could still be reality for me.

Battlecreek Ranch

The cattle drive ended at Battlecreek Ranch, owned by John's partners, Larry and Shelly Richtmyer. In addition to charming log cabins built by Larry for the use of ranch guests, the homestead featured a large, weather-beaten barn, probably close to 100 years old, with corrals stretching out behind. The cattle were herded into several of these, then sorted into cow/calf pairs, and yearlings. Diana got in there with Vicky and did a nice job helping with the sorting.

I took the opportunity to record the cacophony that resulted. That marvelous audio clip, with the sounds of hundreds of cattle mooing, and our friends yipping and yelling while working them on the horses, takes me back almost as much as the audio diary I recorded around the campfire.

That evening, inside the drafty old barn, my fellow trail hands dined, drank, and listened to live country music. I stood outside and talked to Larry, who had served as wrangler for my group. I asked him about the off-season lives of the horses we'd been riding.

"Well, Rick," he began, "those horses run wild in the mountains all winter, fending for themselves. Wind blows the snow off the ridges so they can get to the grass just fine. And there are lots of hot springs around here, so they always have water, even when it's forty below."

> The horses ran wild in the mountains all winter, fending for themselves.

I leaned forward to make sure I was hearing him correctly as he continued.

"We gathered up those horses a week or so before you came, trimmed their feet, nailed some shoes on them, and that's pretty much it."

"Wait a second," I said. "You mean, you put me and all these city slickers on a bunch of wild horses?"

"Oh, they're tame enough. They usually settle right down once they get back into the working life," he said. There was a twinkle in his eye.

As that thought rolled around in my head, I suddenly remembered something I'd been meaning to ask Larry.

"By the way, what's the name of my horse, that red roan appy I've been riding all week?"

"Oh, him. I was wondering how you'd do with him," Larry said with a laugh. "That horse was a real handful last year."

"Really?" I said. "And does this handful have a name?"

Larry looked me straight in the eye as he replied, "We call him 'Trouble.'"

Insights

- It's part of every horse's nature to want to stay with other horses.
- Before climbing on any horse, it's important to have a plan for gaining his respect.
- Even domestic horses can fend for themselves remarkably well if given enough land to roam.

TRY THIS

Ride with Purpose

When you first learned to ride a bicycle, you focused on the handlebars and front tire. As your skill improved, your focus moved farther out in front of you, until you no longer thought of the mechanics anymore; you thought of where you were going. It is the same when riding a horse. The sooner you can get your focus off the horse and onto a task or destination, the quicker you'll improve. So find things to do with your horse, activities that will take your mind off riding and onto a job of some kind, even if it is simply a game played on horseback. And when you do ride just for the joy of riding, keep your eyes up and out in front of you, not on your hands or the horse's head.

10 **The Buddy Problem**

Becoming More Important than
the Rest of the Herd

The cattle drive got me to thinking more about working with the horse's
mind to overcome some of the problems people encounter.

Diana's experience with Vicky was typical. Being herdbound, buddy
sour, barn sour, gate sour, or any of the other terms that refer to horses
that want to stay with the herd, is not a problem from
the horse's point of view. The herd is a place of comfort
and safety. Living in herds has allowed the species to
thrive on this planet for a long, long time, so the desire
to be with others of their own kind is not a defect in design. But there is
no doubt that the behavior of a herdbound horse can be a threat to a human trying to use the horse.

> When you are in the
> picture, there is a new
> herd boss in town.

New Rules

One solution that many clinicians suggest is to teach the horse that when
you are in the picture, there is a new herd boss in town. In effect, you
create two sets of rules in the horse's mind: the rules he naturally lives
by when with other horses, and the new rules he lives by when you are
handling or riding him.

One of those new rules is, "When I pay attention to my human, things
are easy; when I pay attention to the other horses, things are hard."

If I were to teach this to Vicky, I would let her go back where she wanted to go—in this case with the other horses—then make her really work when she got there. She would have to trot circles and figure eights, do lots of changes of direction, speed up and slow down. In other words, she would really use her body and "use her air."

When she got winded, I'd take her away from the other horses to rest, maybe 50 feet or so. When she got her air back, she would naturally start thinking about those other horses again. No problem! We'd go right back to them and do the same thing again: work and lots of it, with plenty of hustle. When she got to huffing and puffing, we'd go away to rest, this time 75 feet away. We'd continue doing this, going away a little farther each time to rest. I wouldn't become angry or impatient about how long it took for her to learn the lesson.

> Paying attention to me, whether other horses were around or not, was always a better deal.

With repetition, Vicky would learn that having her mind on the other horses when I was handling her meant more work. Paying attention to me, whether other horses were around or not, was always a better deal. This plays on the fact that horses instinctively want to conserve their energy for when they really need it to escape predators. It's an even more basic instinct than wanting to be with other horses.

All that moving around at a human's direction has another benefit: it impresses upon a horse that the human is really the leader of the team.

Leadership Reminders

Some horses need to be reminded of who's in charge more often than others. Have you ever seen a child running amok in a store, with the parent shopping a few aisles over, seemingly oblivious to the mayhem? Is the parent paying attention to the child? Of course not! The parent is in his own world, with his own thoughts and priorities. Through his behavior, the child is screaming out for guidance.

Horses do the very same thing. Take your horse out on a trail ride and he may jig on the trail, he may try to eat grass along the way, he may follow too closely or act aggressively toward other horses. He may spook at any little thing. He may throw his head and pull at the bit continually.

Often those are habits he's developed over time, simple patterns of behavior for which there are no longer direct causes. But at one time, when he first started doing these things, he was like the child in the store, crying out for guidance and reassurance that you were really in charge.

The way you give that to him when you're riding is by being an active rider, giving a steady stream of input to your horse: speed up, slow down, step left, step right, collect your frame, stretch out your frame. When you keep a horse's mind occupied, he doesn't have much processing power left over to get in trouble.

> When you keep a horse's mind occupied, he doesn't have much processing power left over to get in trouble.

It is often said that the horse has a one-track mind. In other words, he can think about only one thing at a time. This is useful as a teaching device, but of course, we don't know for certain exactly what horses can and can't do inside their minds. Physiologically, their brains are tiny compared to ours, but that in itself doesn't say much. What we do know is that when you keep a horse busy doing things, he tends to be less distracted and worried about the world around him. When you sit like a lump on the horse's back, he begins to look for things to get upset about.

One analogy I've always liked goes like this. Suppose you and your horse are on a bus. When you take control and drive the bus, the horse relaxes and doesn't worry about the bus running off the road. But if you refuse to take the wheel or do a lousy job of driving, the horse will take over and drive that bus because his life is at stake. It's not that he wants to drive but he feels he *must* in order to survive.

Although I believe that most problems with horse behavior are caused by handlers not acting like leaders, there are some cases where the horse's diet plays a big role. Undesirable behavior can be the result of a pent-up need to move and burn calories. More on that later when I get into what I've learned about horsekeeping (see p. 81).

Insights

- It is natural for horses to prefer being with other horses to being with humans.

- Being drawn to the barn or to a gate are simply variations on being herdbound.

- Herd behavior is not acceptable when a horse is with a human.

TRY THIS

Move the Feet

Moving your horse's feet, from the ground or from the saddle, is a cure-all for many behavior problems. If the horse is misbehaving out of fear, it restores his confidence in your leadership because you are asserting yourself as the dominant member of the team. If the root cause is lack of respect for you, it instills some respect. In general, it proves to the horse that you know the score because not just anyone can get a horse to move. He prefers to be in charge of that part of his anatomy because those four feet are his means of surviving another day.

The next time your horse does something you don't like, get him moving those feet: forward, backward, left, and right. Ask him to put some effort into it. If he starts huffing and puffing a bit, so much the better. Nothing gets a horse's attention like a drain on his reserves of energy and air.

11 Regaining Control
The One-Rein Stop

When Thunder and I encountered the string of firecrackers, I had instinctively pulled his head to one side and moved him in a tight circle. I did the same thing, but with an understanding of why, when Trouble tested me on the second day of the cattle drive.

Straightness

That technique of flexing a horse's head laterally as a way of settling his mind is seen over and over in the work of modern horsemen and horsemen of the past. To understand why it works, you have to understand that a horse wants to be straight. He has his greatest power and the most options for how he uses that power when his body is straight. By the same token, bending him takes away power. Bending him a little takes away a little power; a horse can never run as fast traveling on a circle as he can on a straightaway. Bending him a lot takes away a lot of power.

A horse wants to be straight.

The more a horse is bent, the more he has to think about where his feet are. If he is bent a lot, such as when his head is pulled around to one side by the rider, he has to keep crossing one hind leg in front of the other to keep his balance, and that is nearly impossible to do if he is in a reactive or panicked state of mind. He needs to think about what his feet are

You can't do a fancy dance move and run a race at the same time. Neither can a horse.

doing. You can't do a fancy dance move and run a race at the same time. Neither can a horse.

It's very important to note that I didn't say that bending a horse takes away *all* of his power. I can tell you from firsthand experience that a horse can run off with a rider even if his head is bent to one side; it's just harder for him to do. He can't go as far or as fast.

A Tool for Emergencies

Many horsemanship clinicians today advocate that riders learn and practice an emergency procedure called the *one-rein stop*. By pulling the horse's head to one side and holding it there, a rider can usually stop and settle a horse that is becoming agitated or starting to run off. Any discussion of the one-rein stop, however, must make very clear that it has limitations, that there are situations when it may not work. It could even make matters worse.

A case in point happened to me in 2001. It was one of the few times I rode between my accident with Thunder and getting my confidence back on the cattle drive. I was riding Coins, Diana's horse, before we sold him. I had a funny feeling about him from the beginning. He was aloof, as geldings sometimes are, and had that pull-back problem. I also sensed that he could easily take off or start bucking at any moment. Having that expectation in my mind probably made matters worse.

> I yanked on one rein so hard that it dropped Coins to one knee.

Coins and I had a nice trot going in a small arena. All of a sudden, he veered to the right and picked up speed on his own. I overreacted. I yanked on the right rein so hard that it dropped Coins to his left knee and nearly threw me from the saddle. I released the rein and Coins got back to his feet. Both of us were shaken by the experience.

This is a perfect example of why we need to *practice* this maneuver. It must come easily and naturally to the rider, almost like a reflex, and not done in a panic. The horse must also be familiar with the feeling and not frightened by it. Done correctly, a one-rein stop is used the instant the rider feels the horse going into a reactive rather than a thinking state of mind. It brings the horse's mind back to the rider. Sometimes a simple tug with one rein does the trick and a full stop is not even necessary.

If you are slow to react, the one-rein stop takes a lot of ground to use because the horse travels on an arc as he slows down. Obviously, you won't always have a lot of ground available to get your horse stopped. So being slow to react simply isn't acceptable. You need to practice the one-rein stop ahead of time so it's familiar to both you and your horse. And when you ride, you need to be alert and ready to use it at any time. If you do both, you will be able to stop your horse quickly and safely in just about any situation.

> If you are slow to react, the one-rein stop takes a lot of ground to use.

Crisis Averted

After the incident when I nearly pulled Coins off his feet, I began practicing the one-rein stop with my mare, Candy. Then I was invited to go trail riding in the Superstition Mountains southeast of Phoenix. It was my first trail ride with Candy so I didn't know how she would behave or how her bare feet would hold up in rocky terrain.

Her feet did just fine and there was only one instance when she spooked. We were riding past a staging area where riders, bikers, and runners would leave their vehicles before heading into the mountains. There was just one car there, and as we rode by, the driver started the engine.

Candy bolted like she was breaking out of the starting gate. I honestly do not remember thinking in the split second that followed. Instantly, I was pulling her head around and melting my body into the saddle. Within two strides, Candy was slowing down. Within another two strides, she was stopped, standing calmly as I flexed her head each direction.

> Candy bolted like she was breaking out of the starting gate.

"Nice stop!" yelled Richard Lupardus, my trail buddy that day. He had spent several years in Clinton Anderson's organization and recognized that I had taken Clinton's preaching about the one-rein stop to heart. And speaking of my heart, it was racing just a bit—there were plenty of cacti and loose footing around there that could have caused problems—but Candy and I were both fine and we finished the ride with no further incidents.

The one-rein stop works on two levels. It robs the horse of power by robbing him of straightness. That's the physical level. On the mental level, it reminds the horse that the human is in charge because the human can control his movement. In the horse's world, nothing is so precious as his ability to move freely when and where he wants. He will never willingly give up that ability; it can only be taken by a more dominant creature, a more dominant herd member, or a predator. Or a horseman who knows what he's doing.

Advanced riders sometimes criticize the use of the one-rein stop, but they are also willing and able to ride bolting horses until they run out of steam.

You may hear criticism of bending a horse laterally, whether flexing him repeatedly as an exercise or using the one-rein stop as an emergency tactic. This criticism most often comes from advanced riders whose priorities are different from those of recreational riders. Advanced riders aren't worried about falling off. Advanced riders are willing and able to ride bolting horses until they run out of steam. That's fine for them, but the rest of us need techniques that minimize the chances of our getting hurt. We need to be able to stop our horses and regain control in emergencies. That's why I use and recommend the one-rein stop.

Insights

- Bending a horse takes away his power.
- Bending a horse's head around to both sides (lateral flexion) should be done each time you mount up.
- The one-rein stop is most effective when practiced ahead of time.
- Some horses will run through a one-rein stop.

TRY THIS

Slow Down a Surging Horse

If your horse wants to go faster than you've asked him to, do not try to hold him back by pulling on both reins. Instead let him commit to the mistake, then stop him with a one-rein stop. In the beginning, you won't cover much ground because you will be continually stopping the horse. But eventually he will realize that he is causing himself more work by not listening to you, and he'll slow down.

12 Baby Sarah
Imprint Training the Newborn Foal

After Coins went off to his new home in Nevada, we had only Candy, a situation I wanted to remedy as quickly as possible. I knew that horses do better mentally and physically when they live in a herd, even a herd of two.

Savannah

Susan Bolin, studio manager at Lambchops, happened to see an ad pinned to the bulletin board at her post office in Waddell, a suburb west of Phoenix. It described an eleven-year-old pinto mare with Parelli training. Savannah was her name and she was a smart, "push-button" horse with lots of experience and a striking sorrel and white tobiano coat pattern. Diana fell in love with her immediately and we bought her.

> It seemed Savannah had recently spent some time with the resident stallion while her owners were away for the weekend.

Savannah's owner was a professional baseball player who liked to do team penning with her in the off-season. One time he was returning from a team penning and his truck broke down. He saddled up Savannah and rode to get assistance across the desert in near total darkness, with no problems. I was impressed when I heard that story.

Another story we heard about Savannah would affect us more directly. It seemed she had recently spent some time with the resident stallion while her owners were away for the weekend. The stallion, Maverisk, was a grandson of multi-time World Champion American Paint Horse Ris Key Business.

Savannah's condition was later confirmed by my good friend and future coauthor, Dr. Robert M. Miller. Dr. Miller is a retired veterinarian known around the world for developing Imprint Training, a protocol for handling and training the newborn foal during its first week of life.

Mud Baby

By mid-March 2003, Savannah was ready to give birth. I had been traveling a great deal, so Diana had lovingly converted one of our covered outdoor stalls into a foaling stall. She had attached sheets of plywood to the corral panels, covered the bare floor of the stall with heavy rubber mats, and covered the mats with straw. The foaling stall was roomy, clean, and dry, an ideal place for Savannah to give birth and for the baby to live its first few weeks.

We were counting down the days, consulting our foaling books regularly to be sure we had everything ready. On the evening of March 16, I got home about 10:00 P.M. and together, Diana and I went to examine Savannah. We saw none of the telltale signs that birth was imminent so we went to bed, leaving Savannah free to move around the other stalls or in the adjoining arena. We kept the foaling stall closed off in order to keep it nice. It had been raining and we didn't want Savannah or Candy dirtying up the stall before the baby came.

> The following morning I saw something I wasn't expecting.

It rained hard that night, and the following morning I was sitting at my desk looking out the window at the horses in their stalls when I saw something I wasn't expecting.

"Diana," I yelled excitedly. "We've got a baby!" I raced outside and as I approached the barn I saw a beautiful little blazed face looking back at me. Standing unsteadily, Sarah greeted me with a squeaky nicker. But something was wrong. Sarah was not with her mother. She was with Candy. I was puzzled but shook it off. There was something I needed to do right away.

"I need to move her to the foaling stall," I said to Diana. While she got the stall gates open, I waded into the mud and touched Sarah for the first time. Carefully, I cradled her in my arms, one arm around her back end and one arm around the front, lifting her as I'd been taught to lift our greyhound dogs. The idea was to contain the legs and put minimal stress on the spine.

When we arrived at the foaling stall, Savannah was waiting for us. Rather than setting Sarah on her feet, I gently laid her on her side as I had seen Dr. Miller do.

The Imprint Training Procedure

For the next few minutes, I bonded with Sarah, gently rubbing her all over, showing her that human touch could feel good. Then I began the other tasks that comprise the Imprint Training method. I took each foot, one at a time, and tapped the bottom, mimicking the sensation of having her feet trimmed or shod in the future. When she struggled, I simply restrained her and kept tapping, quickly and rhythmically, about a hundred times on each foot. I made certain that she had stopped struggling and relaxed completely before I stopped. Dr. Miller had impressed upon me that ending too early, while Sarah was still thinking about flight, would reward her for trying to escape.

When all four feet were done, I began rubbing her body with a plastic bag. Again, I continued until she stopped struggling and relaxed. Next I worked with her nostrils, mouth, and ears, moving a finger in and out with the same sort of rhythmic movement I had used with the feet and body. I was desensitizing her, teaching her that the way to get something scary to go away is to stop moving and relax. This would benefit not only me as her future rider, but also veterinarians, equine dentists, and hoofcare professionals who would need to handle her in the future.

I was teaching her that the way to get something scary to go away is to stop moving and relax.

Because she was young and weak, Sarah could be easily flooded with stimuli until she habituated to them. Flooding is a desensitizing technique that makes the stimulus constant and relentless. There is no escaping it, so the subject's brain finally just ignores it. A frequent example that humans can relate to is the ticking of an alarm clock. When you first hear it you focus on it, but because you can't escape it, your brain eventually begins to ignore it. At that point you have habituated to the clock ticking and you can sleep right through it.

Flooding where a full-grown horse is concerned can be very dangerous because of the animal's strength and speed. The horse is programmed to take flight when he becomes concerned about something. Flooding an adult horse is something only professionals should attempt. Flooding a newborn foal is a whole different matter because the human is at that point stronger than the foal.

The last thing I did with Sarah in that first Imprint Training session was to gently flex her head to one side and hold it there until I felt her relax. When I took my hand away, she remained flexed for a few moments, much as she had been in the womb. This would prepare her for lateral flexion in the future, not only for making her soft and supple when I rode and handled her, but also submissive in attitude. I repeated the flexing on the other side before ending the session.

That first session took about fifteen minutes and then I got out of the way. Savannah had been patiently watching the proceedings, no concern evident. She nuzzled and licked Sarah and after a while, the foal got to her feet. She didn't begin nursing immediately and I formulated a plan for milking Savannah to get those first ounces of milk, containing the nutrient- and antibody-rich colostrum, into Sarah as soon as possible. Before it reached that point, however, Sarah found a teat and began drinking. I breathed a sigh of relief and relaxed for the first time since I'd looked out the window earlier that morning. I found a chair and just sat and watched, grinning from ear to ear.

More Imprint Training sessions followed in that first week of Sarah's life. She learned to halter and lead, to move away from pressure, and to load in the trailer. She also learned that I was the leader of our team. She didn't learn every lesson perfectly. Still, we were off to a great start and I was thrilled.

Imprint Training Mistakes

In what I did with Sarah, I followed Dr. Miller's method to a T, and for good reason. With his half century as a horseman, more than forty years as an equine vet and nearly three decades specializing in the early learning of horses, Dr. Miller knows what he's talking about. One of his great frustrations—which I now share with him—is that so many horse owners use his method incorrectly. It has been fully defined in print, in audio, and in video. It is science, it is training, and it is done a certain way for a reason. Anyone who wants to learn it can easily do so.

> **Dr. Miller knows what he's talking about, and one of his great frustrations is that so many horse owners use his method incorrectly.**

Unfortunately, many people don't. They hear about the method, recognize its value, and think they know how to do it. The most common mistake is one of omission, and it is obvious in the language used. If a horse owner tells me he has *imprinted* his horse, I suspect that he has focused on the bonding step, the part that is so satisfying to us humans. But that is only the first step, channeling the automatic learning built into this precocial species by Nature, this tendency to bond with whatever is moving near the foal immediately after birth. The remaining steps in the Imprint Training method—desensitization, sensitization, and leadership—are presented to the foal as training. They require planning, effort, consistency, patience, and self-discipline just as all horse training does. In short, Imprint Training is not just the warm and fuzzy part everyone so enjoys, it's also horse training scaled down to be appropriate for the youngster.

When only the bonding part is done, the foal loses his natural fear of the human. If that's where it ends, the foal almost invariably becomes a spoiled pet. This needs to be balanced with the leadership step to teach the foal to respect the human's space and accept its leadership. By the same token, desensitization teaches a foal to not overreact to stimuli in his environment. Carried to an extreme, the foal becomes dull to every stimulus. Likewise, sensitization teaches the foal to move away from pressure, to be reactive when asked. Carried too far, the foal overreacts to everything.

In Imprint Training, the bonding is balanced by the leadership training, and the desensitization is balanced by the sensitization. The foal receives, in his first week of life, the essential knowledge he will need for his entire life with humans. Best of all, because this is a critical learning time for horses, the foal learns quickly and with great permanence.

No one should be intimidated about using Imprint Training. It is not difficult to perform, and if you do all the steps, to the best of your ability, you will get good results.

My experience with Sarah immediately after her birth was immensely rewarding. Then something happened that threatened to derail all of our progress.

Insights

- Imprint Training is much more than caressing and reassuring a foal.

- The four phases of Imprint Training are bonding, desensitization, sensitization, and leadership.

- The Imprint Training regimen must be studied to be performed correctly.

- Imprint Training produces positive results that last a horse's lifetime.

TRY THIS

Learn Imprint Training

Whether you plan to have foals in the near future or not, learning Imprint Training is time well spent. Dr. Miller's video, audio, and book not only explain this training regimen, but also the reasoning behind it, which is founded on the behavior and fundamental nature of the horse. Those things don't change from the day a horse is born until the day he dies.

13 Needles and Pens
Treating and Training the Young Horse

In spite of all our preparations and best intentions, Baby Sarah had been born in the mud while we slept, snug and dry, a hundred feet away. She seemed none the worse for wear, but our vet was concerned about a systemic infection. I treated the stump of her umbilical cord with iodine—a common procedure for newborn foals—but something more was required. There was no avoiding it. Baby Sarah needed a course of antibiotic shots. And I had to give them to her.

Baby Sarah needed a course of antibiotic shots. And I had to give them to her.

First Shots

Our vet showed me how and where to administer the injections. He suggested that Diana assist by holding Sarah still, but I found that a bit awkward. Then I remembered Dr. Miller once showed me how he gave foals shots all by himself, and I went with that method instead. I took all of this very seriously, as our vet had emphasized the importance of injecting this medicine into a muscle and not a blood vessel. Here's the procedure I used to give Sarah a shot in her left rump muscle:

1   I removed my belt and refastened it to form a loop.

2   I slipped the loop over Sarah's head and down to the base of her neck.

3 Facing Sarah's back end, I slipped my right arm through the belt until the belt rested against my bicep and my right hand was at Sarah's hip.

4 I pulled straight up on her tail with my left hand until her feet were almost off the ground.

5 I gave the injection in the muscle near her left hip with my right hand.

Pulling up on the tail acts somewhat like a twitch on a horse's lip; it may even cause an endorphin release. I don't think anyone knows for sure why it works, but the foal tends to quiet down, allowing the shot to be given with minimal commotion and no hard feelings at all.

By the time I had given Sarah her last shot a week later, I was quite proud of myself, especially since it didn't seem to affect my relationship with her. Three years later, Sarah would have a touch of pneumonia and I would need to give her four shots each day in parts of her body where no horseman wants to be sticking needles. I had no problems and I like to think that somehow she remembered that I didn't hurt her before.

As Sarah grew, she showed one characteristic in abundance: curiosity. No matter what I was doing, if she could see me, she would get as close as she could and watch me intently. If she was in the arena, which doubles as turnout area, she would poke her head through the rails of the arena fence. If she was in the grass paddock at the front of our property, she would hang her head over the fence. If it was getting toward feeding time, she would remind me with an occasional nicker not to forget her dinner. But even in the middle of the day, she was still interested in what I was doing.

> **I decided that I would not start Sarah under saddle until she was at least three years old.**

Starting Sarah under Saddle

I decided that I would not start Sarah under saddle until she was at least three years old. I had heard too many stories about young horses being hurt by being trained too hard too early. But when Sarah turned three, I was busier than ever with live appearances, my radio shows, and ramping up my TV show. Plus, I still wasn't entirely sure I was ready to start a colt. A lot of people stumble through it, but doing it correctly is an advanced skill. I wanted to be correct. I began paying extra attention to the colt-starting demonstrations I saw and visualized doing it with Sarah.

Sarah's three-year-old year slipped by and before I knew it she was four. There's nothing wrong with waiting to start horses but every year they get stronger and more set in their ways. I found that to be true of Sarah.

Having had the most exposure to the colt-starting methods of Clinton Anderson, I felt most comfortable going that route. I followed his ground-work exercises exactly and had great results. But when it came time to ride, I had to adapt his method to my situation. Clinton recommends that the first riding session be done in the round pen with one person on the ground controlling the horse's speed and direction with a flag, and the rider simply holding on, serving as a passenger. Once this is going well, the rider takes over controlling the horse. With Clinton's method, the person on the ground must have the better timing and feel. The person riding has to be experienced and comfortable enough riding to remain in the saddle if anything unexpected happens. I didn't have a second person to help me.

Against this advice, I rode Sarah by myself.

Thus, against this advice, I rode Sarah by myself. I was nervous, and wore a helmet just to be safe, but we had no real problems. She is a smart little horse and I didn't need to be heavy-handed for her to get the message. Plus, she reacts well to my voice. When I praise her for something done well, she seems to understand. When I reprimand in a sharper tone of voice and use the word, "NO!" she gets that, too.

Not long after I had started riding Sarah, we shot a TV episode with Mike Kevil, a great trainer in the Phoenix area who is well known for his colt-start-

After the first two days, it became a battle every time to get the bit in Sarah's mouth.

ing talents, about the importance to a horseman of having both timing and feel. The plan was to use both Candy and Sarah to illustrate his points. Mike was very complimentary about Candy's lightness and responsiveness (plus her coppery coat and perfect blaze looked fantastic on camera).

Sarah was a little more difficult to handle, but under Mike's hand she progressed nicely and got another good riding lesson.

At the time of this TV shoot, Sarah had still not had a bit in her mouth. I had ridden her with a rope hackamore, a modified version of the traditional vaquero-style hackamore. I told Mike that she hadn't been bitted and after the shoot, he spent some time getting her to accept the bit. I began working with her the next day on my own, repeating Mike's lesson. The first two days, she accepted the bit just fine. But after that, it became a battle every time to get the bit in her mouth. Tossing her head and clamping her teeth shut, Sarah did everything she could to thwart my efforts. I knew it was something I was doing, but I couldn't figure out what.

> **When you reach an impasse, go on to something else and come back to the problem area later.**

Slowing Down

About that time, I purchased Tom Dorrance's video, *Greetings from Tom Dorrance*. There was one particular passage that seemed to be meant for me. Tom recommended that when you reach an impasse, don't force the issue; go on to something else and come back to the problem area later. Things will probably be easier then, and the original problem might even be gone.

The next day I decided to try something different. Instead of trying to get Sarah to take the bit in her mouth, I shifted to getting her to accept the headstall rubbed all over her face and held there, with the bit resting on her nose. I also made my top priority not scaring her. I would take whatever time it took.

Over the course of the next few weeks, I worked with her a little every day, occasionally offering the bit by placing it against her teeth and holding until she took some part of it into her mouth. Finally one day, she took the bit in her mouth and I let her carry it for a while, all the while praising her and giving her a good brushing. I wanted carrying the bit to be a positive experience for her. After that, it became a little easier every day.

I thought it ironic that the particular headstall and bit I was using was one I had gotten from Pat Parelli. I was putting into practice Pat's idea about, "polite and passive persistence practiced in the proper position."

The time I spent with Sarah getting her to accept the headstall and bit was special for several reasons. Initially, I put her in a halter with a lead rope attached and kept firm hold of her. Eventually, I dropped the lead rope on the ground. Then I started working with her without any headgear at all. She was completely free to leave at any time. Yet she chose to stay. I trusted her and she trusted me.

When she would move her head away, I got to where I didn't get upset. It wasn't just controlling how I acted; how I felt inside really changed. I would gently move her head back into position with a couple fingers. I talked to her in a calm voice as we did all of this. The use of my voice was not only soothing to her; it kept me calmer, too. Occasionally, she would take a step backward and I would simply touch her on the side, behind the cinch area, and she would step forward calmly and willingly.

PRETEND YOU DON'T WANT IT

Feeding treats to reward desired behavior is a time-honored way of training many animal species. But, as with anything else, it must be done correctly to be safe and effective. Novice horse owners some times end up reinforcing the wrong behaviors or getting hurt.

To avoid that, there is one absolute rule: *A treat must never be given to a horse that is being pushy or disrespectful.* The horse must be taught immediately that impatience will delay getting the treat.

I play a game with my horses called, "Pretend you don't want it." I make certain the horse knows I have a treat. Once she is alert, paying attention, and standing back at a respectful distance, I will hold the treat in front of me and say, "Pretend you don't want it." The horse will look away, as if she has no interest at all in the carrot, or piece of apple, or horse cookie. I will then say, "Good girl!" and she will carefully take the treat from my hand.

Candy is so into this game that she will begin looking away before I've asked her to. That's why I always make sure we start with the horse's head forward. Anticipating the trainer's command isn't desirable even if it's to do something good.

I've found that food can be used very effectively in training horses, and it's not just giving them treats. At feeding time, a horse is very tuned into the one doing the feeding. It's a golden opportunity to teach manners. I'm always surprised when I hear of people whose horses run them over at feeding time. With just a little bit of assertiveness, patience, and consistent enforcement of the rules, you can get a horse to step back and wait respectfully to be fed.

The time spent with my horses in doing the little things is perhaps the most satisfying of all the interaction I have with them. And I know without a shadow of a doubt that it's propelling me forward on my journey, making me more of the kind of man a horse would consider a real partner.

Insights

- Giving a horse an injection is not as difficult as it first seems.

- If a training task is not going well, it is better to try something different and come back later to the problem task.

- In most training situations, scaring the horse should be avoided.

- Food can be an effective reward for desired behavior.

TRY THIS

Touch with Love

I like what Pat Parelli says about the way to touch your horse, "Rub your horse with your heart in your hand." Think about this as you touch your horse. Try to make your affection come through in your touch. And *never* pat or slap the horse. Always stroke, or caress the horse. Do it slowly and gently, but make solid contact. See if you can calm the horse with your touch.

14. Chasing Tom
Internalizing the Dorrance Principles

It was shortly after I started my radio show that I began hearing the name Tom Dorrance. It was always spoken with reverence, as though this was the one man living today who truly understood horses. Some people spoke of knowing him personally, others of being at clinics with him, and others still of the principles he espoused. *People Magazine, The New York Times,* and countless horse publications had done stories on him. Although Pat Parelli had coined the term, "natural horsemanship," it became clear to me that Tom Dorrance was the embodiment of the natural horseman. I think even Pat believed that.

> **Tom Dorrance was the embodiment of the natural horseman.**

Book Learning

Being a reader, I was thrilled to find that Tom had a book, *True Unity: Willing Communication Between Horse and Human.* Technically, Tom didn't write it. Milly Hunt Porter, the ex-wife of Tom's best student, Ray Hunt, put words to paper. It was her attempt, she said, to preserve Tom's work for her grandchildren and everyone else's grandchildren. Tom seemed pleased with the result.

Imagine my disappointment when I first read the book, or rather, tried to read it. It was in English. The grammar, punctuation, and sentence structure were fine. But somehow I couldn't grasp what was being said.

I tried Ray Hunt's book, *Think Harmony with Horses*, and Pat Parelli's book, *Natural Horse-Man-Ship*. Same thing. These were fine books by important horsemen, but my brain just wasn't absorbing the essences they were communicating. "Something must be wrong with me," I concluded. What I didn't realize was that I just wasn't ready. I wasn't far enough along on my journey to understand what they were really getting at.

In the years that followed, I occasionally went back to Tom's book and gave it another try. Slowly the haze began to lift. One of my first insights was that there are no clear-cut answers. If Tom was a bit vague or simple or imprecise in his language, it was because horsemanship is not a cut and dried science. In his video, *Greetings from Tom Dorrance*, he zeroed in on the problem by saying, "There's such a variation of situations that you can't say, 'Do this and you get that.' People have to rely on themselves. I tell people that it has to come right out of the inside of themselves, the end result. There can be some direction, or support and encouragement, but the feel itself can come from no one but themselves; they will know when the feel actually becomes effective, and when they are understanding."

> "There's such a variation of situations that you can't say, 'Do this and you get that.'"

Nuggets of Wisdom

There are a group of observations and suggestions attributed to Tom Dorrance that, even on first reading, were immensely valuable to me. I'd like to share my thoughts on a few of them.

- *Observe, remember, and compare.*
  To me, Tom is saying you have to be mentally engaged when working with horses. You need to be focused on what's going on and apply mental energy as well as physical energy to the process. Every experience you have will add to your understanding, but you need to think about it.

- *Make the wrong things difficult and the right things easy. Let your idea become the horse's idea.*

This is Tom's straightforward way of describing the secret to all animal training, what behaviorists call Operant Conditioning. Desirable behaviors (right things) are rewarded (made easy) and undesirable behaviors (wrong things) are punished (made difficult). Regardless of the words you use, you are setting up a situation and allowing the horse to choose his own outcome. A horse learns very quickly to choose things that give him the best outcome, which is what you wanted all along.

- *Be as gentle as possible and as firm as necessary.*
  It is in this, perhaps the most defining of Tom's ideas, that the concept of justice is seen. An analogy that comes to mind is what it takes to boil water. At sea level, water boils at 212 degrees Fahrenheit. That is the minimum amount of heat that it takes to get the job done. Water will also boil at 213 or 214 or 215, but that is more heat than necessary. Water will not boil at 211 or 210. That doesn't get the job done. Justice where a horse is concerned is the commitment to using the least amount of heat (pressure) necessary to get the job done.

  This is also probably the most misunderstood principle in natural horsemanship because many people only see the gentle part. It feels good to be gentle to a horse, but closing your eyes to the necessity of being assertive and strong at times is foolish and naïve. The horse is more comfortable—in human terms, happier—with a competent leader in charge.

- *The slower you do it the quicker you'll find it.*
  This means a couple of related things to me. One, practicing anything slowly is the way to master it. Speed comes naturally. Two, when things aren't going well, you may be going too fast for the horse, he can't process it that quickly, or the quality of your presentation is suffering because you are racing through it. Slowing down allows you to be better and the horse to keep up with what you're asking him to do.

- *Feel what the horse is feeling and operate from where the horse is.*
  This is nothing more or less than empathy, imagining what another creature, man or beast, must be feeling at a given moment. Putting yourself in the horse's place is not only the moral high ground, it also helps you see solutions you wouldn't otherwise see. Can you really know what it's like to be a horse? Not really. But as a human, you have the ability to think in the abstract, to imagine what it might be like and that gets you close enough.

- *Do less to get more.*
  This is perhaps the most counter-intuitive of Tom's prescriptions, yet I've seen it proven over and over again. The horse's survival instinct is strong, and it is so near the surface in many horses, that it interferes with them learning. Backing off, turning down the pressure, doing less in whatever form it takes, allows the horse's preoccupation with his own survival to lessen and his thinking to increase. Just as with the slowing-down suggestion, doing less may also improve the quality and accuracy of your performance, as well.

- *Take the time it takes.*
  Just as the horse is preoccupied with survival, the human is preoccupied with time. When you are worried about the amount of time a task takes, your body telegraphs it loudly and clearly to the horse. Rather than speeding up the process, worrying about time inevitably slows it down because it worries the horse, too. Conversely, letting things unfold at their own rate usually makes them go faster because the horse does not become worried about his safety.

- *The horse has a need for self-preservation in mind, body, and spirit.*
  This goes to the essential nature of the horse, the nature that the horseman tries to use instead of fight. But it speaks to more than physical self-preservation; Tom invites us to think of the horse as

a complex creature whose mind and spirit must be preserved and protected just as his body is.

- *The horse is never wrong.*
  This last point is wonderfully rich. If you accept this premise—that the horse is never wrong—then you must ask yourself about the real nature of this journey from human to Horseman. The horse doesn't need changing, so it can't be about training horses.

  The journey from human to Horseman can only be about one thing: changing ourselves. It is a course in self-improvement for human beings. At the individual level, it makes humans more effective with horses and with people. At the macro level, it has implications for all mankind. By molding a new, more fully realized human being, we improve the lot of our species and our planet.

  I expressed the idea once this way:

  > **The journey from human to Horseman can only be about one thing—changing ourselves.**

  > This new person observes, remembers and compares. He listens more and talks less. He takes responsibility rather than assigning blame. He controls his emotions. He becomes aware of his body language. He tries to improve himself. He commits himself to acting justly. He cultivates patience. He forgives. He lives in the moment rather than stewing over the past or waiting for the future. And of course, he places the wants and needs of another living creature ahead of his own.

  > From *The Revolution in Horsemanship and What It Means to Mankind* by Robert M. Miller, DVM, and Rick Lamb (Lyons Press, 2005)

Knowing Tom

Tom Dorrance was born in 1910 and died in 2003. He grew up on a cattle ranch in Oregon and his insights into horse behavior came out of the practical needs of a working cowboy. He also understood cattle and how to motivate their behavior. And of course, he understood human nature.

He was a gentle man and a gentleman. Although Tom wasn't inclined to impose his thinking on anyone else, he was generous with his time when asked for help. He often expressed concern that the student not be hurt.

Tom wasn't inclined to impose his thinking on anyone else.

"You're too precious," he would say as he offered a suggestion on a safer way to get something done.

I did not know Tom personally. Perhaps not knowing him accounts in some measure for my fascination with this man. Many people who did know him have told me stories about him. I've talked on several occasions with his widow, Margaret. I've read his book and viewed videos in which he was featured.

Tom Dorrance has become a near-mythical figure, a patron saint to those of us on this journey. It wasn't his intention. He didn't create a body of knowledge or a teaching system or a template for an ideal horseman. He couldn't do

He refused to name his brand of horsemanship.

that any more than I could. What Tom Dorrance did was give us things to think about that help on the journey.

Tom didn't like labels. He refused to name his brand of horsemanship and seemed to resist any attempt to sum it up or delineate its principles. It was just about the horse and the human, and the quest to communicate and become partners. The journey.

Perhaps deconstructing Tom Dorrance is time wasted. He was much loved by his family and friends, and is sorely missed, but he was, in the end, a flesh and blood human like the rest of us. Still, more than anyone of his time, he captured and preserved and passed on something very special, the spirit of the Horseman.

A dose of Dorrance is an effective antidote to complacency and self-satisfaction on one's journey.

Insights

- Horse training is not a cut and dried science.

- A trainer must be both disciplined and flexible.

- Every horse, human, and situation is unique.

TRY THIS

Read Dorrance and Hunt

The books written by Tom Dorrance and Ray Hunt belong in the library of every human who aspires to being a Horseman. It's important to read them, and reread them as you progress on your journey. Their meaning will unfold more with each reading.

15 Death in the Alley

Accepting Responsibility for a Horse's Life

After our kids grew up and moved out, Diana and I fell into a daily schedule that fit our natural rhythms. I would work at the studio in the afternoon and evening, but I preferred to spend mornings at home, puttering around the house and barn, playing with my horses, exercising, reading, and writing. That's why I was home one Thursday morning in October of 2003.

Emergency in the Neighborhood

The doorbell rang about 9:00 A.M. When I opened the door, a distraught young woman I didn't recognize stood before me.

"Is that your horse trailer?" she asked, referring to the two-horse Featherlite peeking over my back fence.

"Yes. What's wrong?" I asked.

"Can you help me get my horse to the vet? I think she's dying!" Her face contorted and tears began streaming down her cheeks.

> "Can you help me get my horse to the vet? I think she's dying!"

"Of course," I said, grabbing my keys. "Where is she?"

"In the alley beside my grandpa's house, that house down on the corner," she said, pointing south. I knew the house. It was on Paradise Lane, which was truly ironic considering what I was about to see.

The woman took off down the street, half running and half walking, rubbing the tears from her eyes as she went. I hooked up my trailer and drove straight to the alley. A second, younger woman was waiting there and waved me toward a light gray mare lying on the ground among the weeds, her head propped awkwardly against a concrete block fence. The crying woman stood nearby.

As I got closer, I saw that the horse was still alive but was struggling to breathe. The head position didn't help and I was just about to suggest that we try to move her when I saw the gray duct tape on her neck. Blood seeping around the edges told me the duct tape was a makeshift bandage intended to seal a wound, a wound that most likely had severed the mare's windpipe.

> The wound most likely had severed the mare's windpipe.

Trying to comprehend how this could have happened and what I could possibly do to help, I heard the horse draw her last breath. She passed away at my feet with no fanfare, no drama. One moment she was alive and the next she was dead. The crying woman let out a wail and began pacing back and forth. The younger woman, who I found out later was her sister and a veterinary student, tried to comfort her.

In the minutes following the horse's death, I pieced together what had happened. The gray mare, one of several nondescript horses and miniature horses kept by the grandfather in a primitive setup next to his home, had sustained the injury sometime during the night. She was on her feet but losing strength rapidly when the older sister found her. When the woman tried to examine the wound, the mare had panicked and broken free, heading down the adjoining alley a short distance before collapsing in the spot where I found her. The younger sister had done what she could to patch the wound, using all she could find in Grandpa's garage, a roll of gray duct tape.

When it became clear there was nothing I could do, I mumbled my condolences and walked back to the truck. The horse's body lay there in the sun for several more hours before someone disposed of it.

Afterthoughts

At the time of the mare's death, I felt nothing but sadness, both for the horse and for the sisters, but later a different feeling began to grow. It was part anger and part frustration. Horses can get hurt and die in just about any situation. For as big and strong as they are, they can at times be very fragile. Even the best-designed facility is not immune to equine injuries and fatalities. I've seen a healthy horse drop dead of a brain aneurysm in a perfectly safe arena in front of hundreds of people. I've seen a yearling show horse rear up while getting his picture taken, fall over backward, and die minutes after winning a halter class. Who can you blame for those things? Nobody.

Horses can get hurt and die in just about any situation.

But that was not the case here. I had noticed this place before and marveled at the disparity between the care given the home and the care given the horse facilities. The house was modest but freshly painted and neat. A sturdy block wall enclosed the back yard. The landscaping, especially one giant desert pine tree spreading over much of the front yard, was beautiful and well maintained. On cold winter nights, bed sheets were painstakingly draped over the smaller plants to keep them from freezing. The grandfather clearly took a lot of pride in his home.

Rusty pipes were lashed together to form a crude corral that sagged and leaned just a few feet from the street.

The animal area was a different story. Rusty pipes were lashed together to form a crude corral that sagged and leaned just a few feet from the street. Stalls formed of wire mesh and wood, and covered with corrugated tin, provided a bit of shade at the back of the lot. None of the attention to detail seen in the home was evident. In fact, everything seemed haphazard and half-hearted, and the potential for injury was everywhere. The lot was an eyesore in the neighborhood and I always felt uneasy about the animals' safety when I drove by.

After the death of the mare, the horse lot remained much the same for several more years. Then one day, the corral and stalls were gone and the foundation for a new house was being poured. Today, a happy young family lives there. I doubt that they know what happened in the alley behind their house on a Thursday morning in October. But I doubt that I'll ever forget.

Insights

- Horses can be injured in almost any setting.

- Chances of injury skyrocket when flimsy materials, sharp edges, and protrusions are found in horsekeeping areas.

- Many horse owners do not know what constitutes safe horse areas.

- A horse that is hurt may not allow you to help him.

TRY THIS

Horse-Proof Your Property

Most hazards that threaten the health and well-being of horses are insidious, meaning they sneak up on us. A nail that has slowly worked its way out of the wood, a piece of tin that is bent to expose a sharp edge, leaves from a toxic plant that have blown in from the neighbor's yard. Once a week, walk your horse property with your eyes open for those kinds of hazards, and fix them. And bear in mind that horses sometimes get out of their stalls, so the surrounding area should be safe as well.

16 At Home with Horses
Creating a Horse-Friendly Facility

For me, the death of the gray mare was a clear reminder of the importance of good horsekeeping. There are plenty of challenges to caring for an animal that was designed to roam freely in herds but the basics of keeping a horse safely and sanely are easy enough to implement, regardless of your situation.

Our situation is a good example. As much as we like the idea of living in a rural area on a horse ranch with sprawling grassy pastures, that doesn't fit our lifestyle any more than living in a high-rise condominium. For us, living in the city on a small horse property is a good compromise.

We live with three horses on an acre-and-a-half within the city limits of Phoenix, Arizona, the sixth largest city in the country. Our horses have plenty of room to move around. They've never had colic and never been injured seriously. They look good and act perfectly happy. They have no behavior problems to speak of. When I'm home, I care for them by myself. It takes about thirty minutes per day to care for my three horses, and that includes picking up all the manure. Training and riding time are extra, of course.

> It takes about thirty minutes per day to care for my three horses.

Preparation

It's no accident that this little place works so well for us. It took six years of planning and preparing our property before we felt we were ready to bring horses onto it.

Our labor of love began at breakfast one Sunday morning back in 1995. The kids were off with friends and Diana and I had our four-bed-room-with-a-pool, quarter-acre, cookie-cutter, suburban tract home to ourselves.

"Still want a horse?" Diana asked, peeking over the top of the newspaper.

"Of course … why do you ask?" I replied. I'd been visiting boarding stables and looking at ads for horses lately. My longtime fantasy of having a horse was intensifying and she knew it. Diana often joked that it was my midlife crisis and she was just happy it wasn't sports cars and younger women. Truth be told, she'd always liked horses, too, and the idea of be-ing horse owners was growing on her.

"Well, we could buy a horse and board him somewhere. That would be expensive and you'd be gone from home a lot," she began. We'd already been down this path. With three kids to educate and a business to run, we had neither extra time nor money for that. Plus, I wanted to be with my horse every day. Boarding him would be like sending my child off to boarding school. I knew I would miss too much.

"Or," she continued, "We could just buy a horse property. Then you could keep your horse at home."

"Uh … who are you and what have you done with my wife?" I deadpanned.

She ignored me and went on. "It could be lateral move. We could sell this house and buy an older one on an acre or so, maybe a little farther out. Here look at this." She tossed me the classified section with an ad circled. It was for a realtor named Peggy Robinson.

"Specializing in horse property in North Phoenix and Scottsdale," I read out loud. I let the idea roll around in my head for a moment, then reached for the phone.

"What the heck? Let's see if Peg works Sundays."

It was no surprise that I got an answering machine, but Peggy's voice was pleasant enough and I decided to leave my name and number at the

Photo 1 Inducting Pat Parelli into the Western States Horse Expo Hall of Fame in 2007 with expo owner Miki Cohen.

Photo 2 Thunder was very forgiving of my ineptitude, even at something as simple as leading him.

Photo 3 Heading out for a ride in the desert on Mandy, Al Raitano's good Quarter Horse mare, around 1996.

Photo 4 An early publicity shot for my radio show.

Photo 5 Pat and Linda Parelli drew a standing-room-only crowd when
I interviewed them at the Minnesota Horse Expo.

Photo 6 Coins getting his pre-purchase exam at the Parelli International Study Center in Pagosa Springs, Colorado.

Photo 7 This was the day I met Candy. She was five, and I was…older.

Photo 8 Coins and I taking a break in the round pen. Neither of us looks too happy. My right pinky finger is still in a splint.

Photo 9 My mount for a week of driving cattle in 2002 was an Appaloosa ranch horse named Trouble.

Photo 10 Driving cattle on Trouble in Montana, June of 2002.

Photo 11 Diana and Vicky get busy sorting cows and calves on the last day of our Montana cattle drive, 2002.

Photo 12 A perfect Sunday ride near home—Diana is on Savannah and I'm on Candy.

Photo 13 Sarah's birthday, March 17, 2003.

Photo 14 Savannah and Baby Sarah in our front
paddock. The neighbors loved to see them out there.

Photo 15 Lynn Palm visited our new horse property in Phoenix and posed with Candy and me.

Photo 16 Dr. Bob Miller and I signing books in California, 2005.

Photo 17 Celebrating with Bob and Debby Miller, and Hugh and Ruth Downs after the release of *The Revolution in Horsemanship and What It Means to Mankind.*

Photo 18 A morning workout—cantering on Candy.

Photo 19 Candy and I relax with Clinton Anderson at the end of our riding clinic, 2004.

Photo 20 Before the First International Equus Congress began we visited a neighboring English camp for kids, Brazil, 2006.

Photo 21 Argentinean horseman Oscar Scarpati Schmid
working with a young mule in Brazil. He redefined trust for me.

Photo 22 With John and Jody Lyons at the Western States Horse
Expo in 2005. Yes, John is riding a donkey.

Photo 23 Monty Roberts and I pose after our first radio interview, around 1998.

Photo 24 At Road to the Horse 2007 with winner Chris Cox and producer Tootie Bland.

Photo 25 Live on RFD-TV with Clinton Anderson. I learned a lot about horse training from him.

Photo 26 Late night picking in Sacramento (from left, "Cowboy" on mandolin; me, Jay Casmirri, and Pat Parelli on guitar; and Rick Swan on bass).

Photo 27 Catching a sunrise in the desert with my American Quarter Horse mare, Candy.

beep. Shortly after noon she called back and two hours after that, Diana and I were pouring over a computer printout of houses that met our search criteria.

The first house we visited was an older ranch-style house on an acre-and-a-half about a mile from where the SR51 freeway was being built. The location was good. The house was long and low with six bedrooms, five baths, and a detached two-car garage. It had been remodeled and expanded at least twice in its twenty-three-year life, and had some odd features owing to a brief period as a nursing home. There were no horse facilities but plenty of room for them. We marked the house as a possibility and moved on to visit seven or eight other homes that afternoon. When the light began to fade, we drove back to the first house and parked in front.

We marked the house as a possibility and moved on.

"I don't know. This might be it," I finally said.

"I know," Diana said.

A few weeks later, around the beginning of August, we were moving in. There's an unwritten rule about living in Phoenix: you always move or undertake major outdoor projects during the hottest part of the summer. Nobody plans it that way; it just always works out that way. Our move proved the rule once again.

Before long, Diana and I had agreed on a basic layout for the future horse facilities. The lot was 200 feet wide and 300 feet deep. The house was in the front left corner, so there was room in the back for a barn and arena, and room in the front for a grassy turnout. The first thing I did was plant Eucalyptus trees around the arena area. They would grow quickly and provide some nice shade.

Three years later came the barn. In the desert, shade and airflow are everything, so barns are often of an open-air design. Our barn had a wash rack, enclosed tack room, and feed room on one side of the breezeway, and three stalls built of corral panels on the other side. Each stall was 12 feet by 28 feet, with half of it covered and the other half open. Each stall connected to the arena, providing plenty of room for the horses to move around. Automatic waterers were in each stall and at one end of the arena.

When we finally brought our horses home in 2001, they moved into the Horsey Ritz.

Next we got the pasture area enclosed with white three-rail polyethylene fencing and I planted a special blend of grass seed designed for horse pastures. An automatic waterer was installed there, too. During the next three years, we acquired a horse trailer, saddles, and various tack. When we finally brought our horses home in 2001, they moved into the Horsey Ritz.

Horsekeeping Education

I was obsessive about all of this, but that's how I approach anything that's important to me. I immerse myself in it. My journey from human to Horseman required me to first realize how little I really knew about horses, not only about how to ride them, but also how to train them, and how to care for them. With a simple trip to a good book store, I found that the information was available. All I had to do was reach out and take it.

The book that meant the most to me as I worked on our property was *Horsekeeping on a Small Acreage* by Cherry Hill. It is one of the most popular of her thirty-some books and videos. Cherry has been on my radio show many times, and she and her husband, Richard Klimesh, have become good friends of ours. We have even visited their private ranch in northern Colorado, where we saw smart, yet simple horsekeeping at its finest.

One thing I've learned is that horses are remarkably adaptable. In training, they often figure out what we want of them even if we do a poor job of asking. They survive and sometimes even thrive in living situations that are dramatically different from life in the wild. They can even get used to being alone, a particular heavy burden on a herd animal. I've also learned that all these things take their toll. Horses become bored and frustrated and stressed much the way humans do. They develop stall vices such as pacing, weaving, cribbing, and wood chewing. They develop antisocial behavior toward other horses and toward humans. And they develop medical problems such as ulcers, colic, and dental issues.

> Horses survive and sometimes even thrive in living situations that are dramatically different from life in the wild.

My horses have not experienced any of this, and I think some credit goes to how we care for them. Rather than giving horses the least I can get away with, I want to give them the most of what they really need. Otherwise, why have them?

Bad Horsekeeping

The gray mare in the alley fell victim to bad horsekeeping born of ignorance. I give the grandfather the benefit of the doubt and assume he just didn't understand how dangerous his setup was. He didn't understand that it constituted a living environment that was almost certain to lead to problems for a half-ton, highly reactive prey animal like a horse. Some horses live their entire lives—or die gruesome deaths as the gray mare did—in such situations. As bad as this one was, it wasn't the worst

Good intentions often live side by side with poor execution.

possible. Often the quarters are also cramped, the manure and flies are overwhelming, and the horse has no company from other animals. At least the gray mare suffered none of that.

It's also possible that the grandfather knew his horse area needed attention and fully intended to make improvements. Good intentions often live side by side with poor execution.

As I learned more about what horses need from us, I saw another form of bad horsekeeping. It came up repeatedly, often among people who I felt should have known better.

Insights

- Horses need the company of other animals.
- A traditional enclosed barn is not the only solution for keeping horses.
- Water must be available for horses at all times.
- Horsekeeping should mimic, as much as possible, the natural life of the horse.

TRY THIS

Evaluate Horsekeeping Setups

As you travel about in your normal life routine, take notice of the environment in which you see horses being kept. Look for what is good and what is bad. How much room does the horse have to move? Are there other animals within his eyesight that can give him the sense of being in a herd? Is the fencing safe? Does he have access to water at all times? Think about how you could fix the problems you see and make a mental note of the good ideas you find.

17 Micromanagers Need Not Apply
Giving Horses the Wrong Kind of Attention

Bad horsekeeping isn't always the result of neglect. In fact, I see just as much of it coming from people doing the opposite. Instead of giving the horse too little attention, the owner smothers him with attention, and it's often the wrong kind of attention. I call this micromanaging.

It Feels Too Good

Horses don't need as much attention from us as most people think. In fact, I've discovered that horses are perfectly happy—or whatever the equine equivalent of happiness is—when we simply leave them alone. This is completely counter-intuitive to most humans. And even if they do understand it, they have a hard time accepting it. For some people, micromanaging a horse just feels too good.

> They lavish upon their horses attention and affection, but accept disrespect in return.

Micromanagers fuss over their horses, blanket them, and protect them from the elements. They shoe them when there is no reason to do so. They give them too many supplements, too many baths, too much clipping, too little exercise, and too much to eat.

Curiously, micromanagers often neglect to teach their horses manners. They do not enforce boundaries in space and behavior. They lavish upon their horses attention and affection, but accept disrespect in return.

Why do people micromanage their horses? Reasons vary but I can give you three big ones: vanity, neediness, and anthropomorphism.

Vanity

Let's consider vanity first. Many people see their horses as reflections of themselves, much the way they see their cars, homes, spouses, children, or jobs. A beautiful horse feeds the ego of his owner. In itself, there's nothing wrong with that. Unfortunately, the beauty the owner seeks is often not the natural beauty of the animal but an artificial, arbitrary human distortion of that beauty that compromises the horse's ability to function in his environment. The show world is responsible for much of this, because in the show world, exaggeration and caricature are often rewarded. Animals that carry to an extreme a physical feature or way of moving often take home the prizes. Recognition means nothing to a horse but it can mean everything to a human.

> The beauty an owner seeks often compromises the horse's ability to function in his environment.

Let me give you some examples that come immediately to mind. In some horse breeds, a smooth head is so highly valued that the owner will remove every whisker on the horse's head, robbing him of feelers that serve as an early warning system to protect his delicate skin and organs, including his eyes.

Many horse owners involved in showing don't like the horse's winter coat so they simply cut it off. Never mind that it has a purpose. Body-clipping a horse in winter precludes operation of the sophisticated thermoregulation system provided by his heavy winter coat, which can be fluffed at will to trap air much like a down ski jacket. Putting a blanket on a horse doesn't solve the problem. Nor does keeping him in a heated barn. He alternately sweats and chills, and the stress that puts him under can easily cause other problems.

> A horse's heavy winter coat can be fluffed at will to trap air much like a down ski jacket.

Tails that serve to swish away flies and communicate to other horses are surgically altered to quiet them, to make them lie flatter, or stand more upright, depending on the breed and what judges like to see.

The examples go on, and become more disturbing when the purpose is to affect a horse's way of carrying himself—from soring the feet for the purpose of making the horse lift his front legs higher and extend them farther, to working him to exhaustion or even draining blood from him to get a lethargic, grotesquely slow gait in the show pen.

Whether it's seen in horsekeeping or horse training practices, micromanaging a horse in this manner is beneath the dignity of the human being. Yet it happens every day. I just can't imagine why people who claim to love horses are so eager to change the very things that make them horses.

Neediness

Neediness is another reason that people mismanage or micromanage their horses. Horses fill needs in all of us. That's why they are so special. It's okay to feel the need to be with your horse. I certainly feel it and can't wait to see my horses when I get home at the end of the day or from a trip. I don't care who sees me hug and kiss my horses. Neediness becomes a problem when it becomes obsessive, when the owner so craves something in return—often something a horse is incapable of giving—that he ignores what is best for the horse.

Excessive bathing is one example. Many horses in boarding stables spend their lives in stalls and are seldom ridden, yet the owners still bathe them regularly. It's an emotional thing, an excuse to caress the horse and coo over him. The fact is most horses don't need to be bathed. They have their own ways of managing their coats. They roll in the dirt. They look grungy for a while but then the dirt wears off, and their coats are shiny. Dirt is like a dry shampoo.

Most horses don't need to be bathed.

I seldom bathe my horses. If they are really filthy and brushing won't do the job, I'll bathe them before riding. Putting tack on a dirty horse is hard on both of them. After riding, my horses are usually sweaty. If I choose to bathe them at that time, it's purely for the bonding time. I know full well that it's not necessary. I also know that just as soon as they can, they will go roll in the dirt, even if they're still wet. It's their instinct and there's a reason for it.

Cleaning out the horse's feet is another example. Think about this logically. Who cleans out the wild horse's feet? Wild horses have superb, hard, healthy feet, so cleaning them out regularly must not be that important in the big picture. And suppose you are with your horse four hours a day, which is a lot for most of us. That's another twenty hours a day that no one is cleaning out his feet. Wild horse studies have suggested that organic matter packed into the horse's hoof actually cushions the foot and thereby serves a useful

> Organic matter packed into the horse's hoof actually cushions the foot and thereby serves a useful purpose.

purpose. Checking your horse's feet regularly and removing any stones stuck there is fine, and is especially important when you're riding, but contantly cleaning out the manure and dirt is not doing him any favors.

One last example is feeding. I'll save most of my comments on feeding until the next chapter, but the point is that neediness drives horse owners to feed their horses not what the horses require for their health and well-being, but what the owners get the most enjoyment out of seeing them eat. When I was growing up, my favorite food in the whole world was my mother's homemade banana cream pie. I'm sure she loved watching me eat it. But she was too smart and loved me too much to give me a steady diet of it.

Anthropomorphism

The final reason that comes to mind for micromanaging a horse is anthropomorphism, or thinking of the horse as if it were a human being. This is a widespread and generally harmless phenomenon that's even seen in names given to inanimate objects, such as B.B. King's guitar ("Lucille"), Pat Brady's windowless jeep ("Nellybelle"), and Davy Crockett's musket ("Old Betsy").

One common example is heated barns. Horses that are allowed to keep their winter coats are quite comfortable at temperatures well below freezing. A cold, drafty barn, especially if it allows the horse to go outside when he chooses, is ideal for a horse's winter quarters. When barns are heated and sealed from drafts, it is for the comfort of humans, who assume it is also in the best interest of their horses. It's not.

Another example is winter feed. A warm bowl of oatmeal may be perfect for us on a cold winter's day, and it's almost irresistible to give a horse the equivalent, a warm bran mash. Yet this does nothing to keep him warm. The best thing to give a horse in winter is more grass hay, free choice if possible. Digesting high fiber food such as hay generates heat from the inside all day long.

All three of my horses have human names: Candy, Savannah, and Sarah. But I never think of them as humans. I love them too much to do that. The differences between our species are that important. It's not just that horses are prey animals and humans are predators. Or that horses are designed to thrive outdoors in weather and terrain that would kill us, or that horses are happiest living in groups and humans are perfectly happy to be alone at least some of the time. There's something else I just can't forget: our brains.

The equine brain is less than half the size of the human brain. Taken as a percentage of body weight, it's one-twentieth the size of ours. Common sense tells us that the quantity and quality of mental activity in these two species is going to be different. I can't say what is going on in the horse's brain, but I'm fairly certain it's different than what goes on in our brains.

Beautiful Jim Key

In our first season on television, we devoted one entire episode to the famous "educated" horse, Beautiful Jim Key (1889–1912), whose story was told so lovingly in the book by Mim Eichler Rivas. I've thought a great deal about what was really going on with that horse.

Beautiful Jim Key was born sickly and was nursed to health by his owner, a self-taught veterinarian, entrepreneur, and former slave named Dr. William Key. They developed an extraordinarily close relationship. They were always together, even at night. The level and quality of communication possible when a human and a horse spend decades in constant companionship, even to the point of sleeping in the same barn within eyesight of one another, may simply be beyond our comprehension. But the story of Beautiful Jim Key is more than a

The horse appeared to be able to read, write, do arithmetic, make change, and sort mail.

horse/human love story. In countless public demonstrations, the horse displayed human-like problem-solving abilities. The horse appeared to be able to read, write, do arithmetic, make change, and sort mail. He even seemed to have a sense of humor and the ability to crack jokes. All of this was said to have been facilitated by the humane, loving care given Jim by his owner, Dr. Key.

"He was taught by kindness," was the catchphrase used by the act's manager, Albert R. Rogers. At a time in history when horses were still working animals, were treated like machines and routinely suffered unspeakable brutality before merciful death claimed them, this was a profound thought. It helped launch the humane movement in America.

But the question remains. Was Beautiful Jim Key—a horse—able to think like a human?

From this distance across time—a century after his public demonstrations ended—there is no way of proving conclusively one way or another. Written records are all that remain, and history has shown us time and again how those can be manipulated to serve a certain purpose or simply fall victim to subjectivity and faulty memories.

The possibilities are tantalizing but I have to remain a skeptic. Horses think like horses, not like humans, and no amount of loving care and training can change that.

Horses and Humans Are Different

Good horsekeeping practice demands that we avoid anthropomorphism, that we accept the differences between our species, that we allow horses to live, to the maximum extent possible, as Nature intended them to live, even if we can't imagine living that way ourselves. When we can't imagine being out in the cold, we have to give them that option. When we can't imagine being covered with shaggy hair, we have to leave it alone. When we can't imagine eating grass hay, we must give it to them. It is not only good horsekeeping, it is the kindest thing we can do for them.

> Do not compound the compromise already inflicted on the horse through domestication by making his life even more unnatural.

Some folks would argue that we have already robbed the horse of his natural life by domesticating and confining him. It's absolutely true. Still, there is much we can do to give a horse his natural dignity, movement, and lifestyle, and still have him in our lives. People do it all the time. I do it every day. It's so simple, folks make it difficult: get out of the horse's way. Let him be a horse. Do not compound the compromise already inflicted on the horse through domestication by making his life even more unnatural. Give this to the horse because it's the right thing to do and because you love this animal, as I do.

Insights

- Pursuing a human ideal of equine beauty can compromise the health of the horse.

- Clipping a horse's winter coat prevents him from warming himself.

- Most horses don't need to be bathed.

- Cleaning manure and dirt out of a horse's hoof isn't always necessary.

- Horses can't give us the kind of affection we sometimes crave.

- Even the smartest horses do not think like humans.

- What is comfortable for a human may not be comfortable for a horse.

TRY THIS

Think Like a Horse

This is a purely mental exercise but the more time you spend around horses, the easier it will be to do. Try to see the world as a horse would. Imagine your world as being filled with predators that would like nothing better than to have you for lunch. Imagine how reactive you would be to sensory input if your primary defense was to take flight.

18 The Need for Forage

Feeding the Horse What He was
Meant to Eat

Horses are beautiful, inspirational, spiritual, exciting, freeing, romantic. They touch us in ways that other animals or recreational activities don't. This is an age-old attraction that is still alive and well, and it has made horses one of the largest industries in America today—$39 billion per year in goods and services at last count.

Shattered Dreams

People become part of the horse industry with dreams and expectations of what it will be like: exhilarating rides, tender moments of bonding, proud moments of accomplishment, and so on.

The problem is that the reality of being around horses is often different from the dream. The reality is that horses test us constantly, they require a lot of work, they are expensive, they are frustrating, and they are dangerous. Sometimes the reality is so different from the expectation that people just get out of horses entirely and go on to something else. Maybe they don't know where to turn for help; maybe they just don't want to put forth that much effort.

> **The reality of being around horses is often different from the dream.**

A major reason humans give up on horses is that they get hurt or become afraid of getting hurt. The behavior of the horse thus becomes a big issue. It's not that we want to control everything about a horse's behavior—the spontaneity and freedom of a horse is part of what we love about them—but we want to control the behavior that threatens our safety.

How do we do that? Part of the solution lies in educating the horse about what is expected of him in his interaction with humans. Part of it is in educating the human with an understanding of equine psychology and horse handling techniques. And part of it is the diet of the horse.

These horses have an abundance of energy and no way to use it.

The horse's diet affects his health and well-being, which can certainly affect his attitude. The diet also determines how much energy he has. Too often, recreational horses that simply stand around most of the time are given feed that is too high in calories and protein, and too low in fiber. These horses have an abundance of energy and a lifestyle that gives them no way to use it. It's no wonder this manifests itself in behavior problems.

You wouldn't give a child a can of soda and a chocolate bar, then ask him to sit quietly through a history lecture. He would be beside himself with energy to burn and it most likely would result in inappropriate classroom behavior. If it was summer vacation and he could run and jump and climb trees and play baseball and act silly to his heart's content, it would be a different matter.

An energy bar that gave you a boost on a hike might keep you tossing and turning all night if you ate it at bedtime. Likewise, a bowl of high-fiber cereal and a bran muffin for breakfast each morning would likely keep your bowels happy under normal circumstances, but would make you miserable if you were suffering from diarrhea. The point is, it matters what we eat and it matters what horses eat.

Why do people feed the wrong things to their horses? I mentioned earlier that it is sometimes neediness, wanting to see the horse enjoy himself the way I enjoy my mother's banana cream pie. Other times, the owner really wants to feed the horse correctly but simply doesn't know how. Unfortunately the handiest source of information—other horse owners—is often the least reliable. At boarding stables, ignorance and misinformation run rampant and it's not limited to just the customers.

People who should know better—proprietors of facilities, trainers, and breeders—are often also ignorant about what a horse really needs.

So what does a horse really need in his diet? The answer is simple: forage, and lots of it.

Grass

Forage is a broad term for what a horse gets in nature. The primary component is grass. Horses are grazers—in other words, they are animals meant to eat grass. Grass that has been cut becomes grass hay. Whether it is growing out of the ground or comes in a bale from the local hay barn, grass should be the mainstay of every horse's diet.

Grass should be the mainstay of every horse's diet.

This isn't just my opinion. I've interviewed dozens of equine veterinarians and nutritionists, people who have devoted their education and professional life to understanding how a horse's digestive system and metabolism work. Each of them has emphasized to me the importance of grass in a horse's diet.

Grass is what the horse's digestive tract, his bowels, his metabolism, his teeth—everything about him—is designed for. The digestive system of the horse is designed to work on small amounts of high fiber food continually throughout the day. The high fiber content of forage acts like a broom to keep his bowels functioning normally. The silica structure in a blade of grass provides abrasion on the horse's teeth, which helps offset the constant growth (technically, eruption) of the teeth throughout his life. The horse can nibble on grass all day long without overeating. This keeps his mind occupied and contributes to his mental and behavioral health. It also reduces the likelihood of developing stomach ulcers because there is always something in his stomach absorbing digestive juices. With his head down to the ground in the grazing position, a horse can even clear his air passages so he can breathe better.

Alfalfa

Many people feed their recreational horses alfalfa hay. This is usually a mistake. Because it is called hay (which simply means it is no longer growing out of the ground) alfalfa hay is often confused with grass hay. They are sold at the same feed stores, they are stacked side by side, and, to the uneducated eye, they look the same.

The fact is, alfalfa and grass are not the same. Not by a long shot. Alfalfa and grass are two completely different plants. Alfalfa (also known as *Lucerne*) is a legume, in the same family as clover, peas, beans, lupins, lentils, and peanuts. Alfalfa is a good source for higher levels of protein, which makes it an appropriate addition to the diet of a workhorse or a horse in heavy training, but the typical recreational horse simply doesn't need alfalfa.

Alfalfa is an appropriate addition to the diet of a horse in heavy training.

But here's the rub. Horses like alfalfa better than grass. A lot better. Some owners simply can't resist seeing their horses gobble up a flake of alfalfa instead of nibbling on a flake of grass hay over the course of several hours.

Sweet feed is another example. It's a mix of various grains and molasses with a high protein and calorie count. Horses love it but most do not need it, and as with alfalfa, they have excess energy that can manifest itself in behavior problems.

With all the reasons I've given you to feed grass hay, I will admit that it is a pain to deal with. It is dirty and sometimes dusty. It leaves a mess where you store it and where you feed your horses. It's hard to give a precise ration, and the quality of grass hay often varies throughout the year. In short, you have to really want to do right by your horse to feed him grass hay.

Some owners choose pellets or cubes instead. These purport to be real grass in a compressed form. Compared to bales of hay, they are much easier to store and to feed, especially when traveling. In my opinion, this is an improvement but still a compromise. The greatest drawback is how quickly the horse finishes his feed. With pellets, cubes, or any kind of packaged feed, the horse is done in minutes instead of the hours it takes him to eat his hay ration. Horses with time on their hands are more likely to get into trouble, same as kids.

In this day and age, there is one thing that the grass we feed our horses can't do. It can't provide all the nutrients a horse needs. Wild horses supplement the grass they eat by eating other plants, bushes, and the bark off trees. They will even eat dirt to get minerals they need. They seem to know instinctively how to get what their bodies need from the world around them.

Domestic horses depend upon us for their nutrition. We can't give them endless natural terrain in which to roam and forage for themselves. Even pasture grass or grass hay can't provide all the nutrients their bodies need due to the depletion of nutrients in the soil where the grass is grown. Thus an educated, conscientious owner has no choice but to supplement the all-important grass with manufactured feed containing the balance of nutrients needed.

This is not a bad thing at all. In fact, to my way of thinking, it's the best of all worlds: science and nature working together to give the horse what he really needs.

To sum up:

- The typical recreational horse that is ridden once or twice a week needs grass hay and an all-in-one packaged feed that is designed to go with grass hay and is appropriate for the horse's stage in life.

- The horse that is in intensive training or works for a living needs the same diet supplemented with limited amounts of alfalfa and grain as needed to give him the additional calories and protein he needs for the work he does.

But all horses, regardless of how they are used, need grass.

Insights

- Horses are grazing animals, which means they are designed to eat grass.
- The high fiber of grass keeps a horse's intestinal tract cleaned out.

- Eating grass keeps a horse occupied and contributes to his mental health.

- The silica structure of grass provides beneficial abrasion to the horse's teeth and offsets the continual eruption of the teeth.

- Horses with adequate grass in their diets have less incidence of colic and stomach ulcers.

TRY THIS

Vary Feeding Times

Although horses are designed to eat grass off and on all day long, most domestic horses have to adapt to being fed twice daily. When feeding times are precise (for example, at exactly 6:00 A.M. and exactly 6:00 P.M.), horses develop an expectation that it will always be that way and some of them become stressed if feeding is delayed by even an hour. I found with my own horses that I could lessen their anxiety by deliberately varying their feeding times over a range of three hours. In other words, morning feeding would be between 6:00 A.M. and 9:00 A.M. Evening feeding would be between 6:00 P.M. and 9:00 P.M. Thus, they developed no expectation about being fed at a precise time; they knew the food would come eventually.

19 Getting It on Paper
Meeting Horsemen of the Past

"Bob, please tell me you're going to do a book on this!" I said.

It was a pleasant winter's day in Arizona, mild and clear. Diana and I were at Queen Valley Mule Ranch and had just heard a lecture titled, "The Revolution in Horsemanship," by Dr. Robert M. Miller. The lecture, laced with clips of video from a stack of VHS tapes, focused on how the natural horsemanship movement had capitalized on the unique characteristics of the equine species and the way it learns.

The year was 2003. By this time I had interviewed Dr. Miller numerous times and had done an audio book with him on Imprint Training, his training regimen for newborn foals. He and his wife, Debby, had become good friends of ours.

"I'd like to do another book, but I just don't have the time," he replied. At 76, he still rode horses and mules, swam every day, and skied each winter. Plus, he and Debby loved to travel. I understood Dr. Miller's reluctance to embark on a big project. His time was just too precious.

The Revolution in Horsemanship

During the next week, an idea formed in my mind. Lyons Press was interested in publishing a book with me. "Maybe the revolution in horsemanship should be the topic of that book," I thought. "And maybe Bob Miller will agree to be my coauthor." Although many books had been written about the techniques and principles of natural horsemanship, none to my knowledge really gave the backstory, the science behind it, where it came from, and the people, past and present, who championed the ideas. It was also something in which I personally believed deeply and actively promoted through my radio shows. Dr. Miller's lecture would be the jumping-off point for the book.

Bearing in mind Bob Miller's priorities, I offered to do the research, procure the photographs, type the manuscript, negotiate with the publisher, and write everything except those chapters he specifically wanted to write.

Dr. Miller accepted my proposal, the publisher accepted him as my coauthor, and we were off and running. Almost immediately, we had the sense that this would become an important book.

The greatest challenge for me, and the part I remember most about writing the book, was digging out historical information on horsemen of the past. A key premise was that the principles underlying natural horsemanship were not new. To support that, I needed to introduce readers to historical horsemen who were committed to working with the horse's mind rather than working over his body. That took lots of research, both online and in old books. I began to buy every old horse book I could find and to borrow others from Dr. Miller.

> A key premise was that the principles underlying natural horsemanship were not new.

Criteria for including a given horseman in the book formed quickly. For instance, there had to be enough material written by or about a person to get a sense of what he was about. Also, since every human is a product of his times, I had to take into account the context in which his work took place. Finally, I had to decide if there was to be a litmus test, one thing that could cause a horseman to be included or excluded regardless of what else I might know about him.

> Empathy: from this one quality flows everything else of importance.

In a sense, I did develop a litmus test: empathy. From that one quality—willingness to try to see the world through another creature's eyes—flowed everything else of importance. If I felt a horseman of the past really tried to understand the nature of the horse and work with that nature rather than against it, a simple expression of his empathy, then that person qualified for inclusion.

There were some jarring inconsistencies. For instance, the celebrated English horseman William Cavendish, aka the Duke of Newcastle (1592–1676), once wrote, "I work on the horse's memory, imagination and judgment, which is why my horses go so well. Forgive him his faults that in the morning he may well know you have mercy as well as justice." Sounds good, doesn't it? Yet on the use of spurs, he wrote, "The shanks of the spurs should be long, the rowels should have six sharp points. When they are used, the blood should flow freely." He also wrote, "I seldom beat them, or punish them with either rod or spur but when I meet with great resistance, and that rarely."

> Cavendish seldom beat or spurred the horse, but when he did, he wanted blood to "flow freely."

Do you see the problem? Pulled out of context, everything becomes confused. Cavendish clearly worked with the horse's mind in a most admirable way. He seldom beat or spurred the horse, but when he did, look out! He wanted blood to flow freely.

I ended up just trying to present as complete a picture as I could of each horseman included. I decided to be neither critic nor apologist and let the reader draw his own conclusions.

Profiling horsemen of modern times presented the same sort of challenges but with some twists. There were some obvious choices about who should be included. But there were also many outstanding natural horsemen who were virtually unknown to the public and, to our surprise, some of them wanted to stay that way. We had to honor their wishes.

I decided that for modern horsemen, I had to go with those who were not only using natural horsemanship but were promoting it through teaching. These were the people who were actively contributing to the growth of this revolution in horsemanship.

The other wrinkle in compiling such a set of profiles was simply my own ignorance. I felt certain there were old-timers as well as up-and-comers that I should have known about but didn't. There would be horsemen that would come to my attention after the book was published that I would sorely regret I didn't include. Dr. Miller and I talked it over and decided to just say that in a short afterword.

Thus, I ended up with seventeen horsemen of the past and seventeen horsemen of modern times. Most readers greatly appreciated the insights these biographical sketches gave them into the lives and work of these horsemen. I took an occasional bit of flack over my choices but nothing serious.

Dr. Miller and I were most interested in the horse training part of this revolution in horsemanship, but our publisher wanted us to expand the scope of our book to include sections on riding, tack, nutrition, medicine, alternative therapies, and hoof care. Dr. Miller wrote the chapters on nutrition and medicine, and I did the others. Each was a learning experience unto itself, requiring a great deal of research and careful writing. But the one I agonized the most about was hoof care.

Hoof Care

I had struggled with the issue of hoof care for my own horses, and I saw that chapter as an opportunity to immerse myself in research and resolve my questions once and for all. As with the rest of my journey, this part produced as many questions as answers.

To horsemen of the past, "No foot, no horse," was like someone today pronouncing, "No wheel, no car."

There is an old saying (and title of a book published in England in 1751) "No foot, no horse." To horsemen of the past, this wasn't a profound thought. It would be like someone today pronouncing, "No wheel, no car." Everyone understood that foot problems could render a horse useless, and that simply wasn't acceptable. Thus, the end goal was always to gain maximum use from the horse.

I found in my research that today, when most horses are used for recreation rather than work, there is a significant split in the horse industry and some fairly heated debate regarding hoof care. On one side are those who advocate leaving horses barefoot and simply trimming their feet regularly. Within this bigger group are factions that disagree on the specifics. For instance, just how should the bare foot be trimmed? How often should trimming occur? What angle should the hoof have relative to the ground? Should the hoof wall be the primary weight bearing structure or should the sole, bars, and frog also bear weight? Should a horse's feet be soaked in water regularly? How does lifestyle fit in? Can a horse that is kept in a stall do as well without shoes as a horse that roams over large pastures with a variety of natural terrain? What about horses with hoof deformities or problems brought about through their care and use, such as laminitis or navicular syndrome? Is therapeutic shoeing ever justified?

On the other side of the argument are people who advocate the use of nailed-on metal shoes. In general, I found this group less dogmatic in its thinking. In other words, most of them recognize that horses are designed to be barefoot and that barefoot vacations—periods in which the horse does not wear nailed on metal shoes—can counter some of the admitted ill effects that come from shoeing. Still, they believe fervently that shoeing some horses in some situations is far more humane than leaving them barefoot. And of course, it makes the horse more usable more of the time.

> Arguments made by either side refer to the natural horse but arrive at very different conclusions.

Interestingly, almost any argument made by either side refers at some point to the natural horse, the horse running wild in nature without man directly controlling his life. Yet, they arrive at very different conclusions about how a horse's foot actually functions.

I was most impressed by a man who seems to live squarely in the middle of all of this, Gene Ovnicek. The first thing that impressed me was that after several decades as a farrier, researcher, and clinician, Gene is still learning about the horse's foot. He is still open-minded enough to learn from every horse he sees.

He recognized that horses should go barefoot if at all possible and he developed a way of trimming the hoof, called the Natural Balance® trim, that reflects what he learned studying wild horses in four dramatically different terrains. All of those wild horses had feet that shared several characteristics, the most surprising of which was that the hoof wall was not the only weight-bearing structure in the hoof. The sole, bars, and frog of the foot bore weight, too. In fact, the hoof wall chipped away in a predictable manner, regardless of the terrain, so that these other structures bore even more weight. Rather than carving them away as some other barefoot trims dictate, Gene recommends leaving those structures on the bottom of the foot full and merely exfoliating any loose or flaking material.

But Gene also recognizes that horses sometimes need shoes and he incorporates his understanding of the equine hoof in a shoe called the Natural Balance® shoe. This horse shoe is characterized by a ridge, set back a bit from the toe, which causes the hoof to function more like a wild horse's hoof than other shoes can.

As with the horsemen whose work I profiled, I decided to just present the various hoof care arguments and let the reader draw his own conclusions.

The Real Importance of the Revolution

Bob Miller and I knew from the beginning that the main title of our book would be, *The Revolution in Horsemanship*. But we wrestled with the subtitle for some time. It was important to us that it convey the greater value we saw in this revolution, beyond just improving the quality of horsemanship practiced by recreational horse owners. We truly believed that the sort of reinventing necessary to make yourself into a horseman was a fine course in self-improvement for individuals. Extrapolated to society at large and on to mankind itself, the implications were staggering.

It's not that we thought natural horsemanship would make the problems of the world go away. But we believed that committing to this philosophy could make for better individuals and that always helps.

Thus the full title of the book became *The Revolution in Horsemanship and What It Means to Mankind*. Chapters 10 and 20 presented this theme in Dr. Miller's words and in my words, respectively. An author isn't always excited about having his words recited back to him. It isn't always meant to be complimentary. However, at one of my public appearances a year or so after the book was published, a gentleman approached me and expressed how meaningful he found the final chapter. When people asked him why he was into horses, he simply asked them to read the words with which I opened chapter 20. He kept them on his refrigerator:

> No one gets into horses to become a better human being or to find greater meaning in life or to make the world a better place, but sometimes that's exactly what happens.
>
> In the beginning, you play with horses because it's fun. It's a pleasant diversion. Then you find that it feels good in a deeper and more lasting way than many other recreational pastimes. You may love riding motorcycles, but your Harley doesn't nicker at you in the morning. There is something very special about horses that makes you want to do better with and for them.

From *The Revolution in Horsemanship and What It Means to Mankind*, by Robert M. Miller D.V.M. and Rick Lamb (Lyons Press, 2005)

People ask me how Hugh Downs, the legendary broadcaster best known for tenures on *The Tonight Show, The Today Show, and 60 Minutes,* came to write the foreword to that book. Dr. Miller and Hugh have been good friends since they met on an Arizona ranch nearly fifty years ago. I became acquainted with Hugh when he started using my studio for his voice recording. Now in his mid-eighties, he's still mentally sharp and his distinctive voice still rings with credibility. Hugh Downs is a true renaissance man, interested in everything around him, including the horse. He wrote the foreword as a favor to Bob and me.

> Legendary broadcaster Hugh Downs is a true renaissance man, interested in everything around him, including the horse.

Insights in Small Bites

Another book project that I had in the back of my mind for some time was very different from *Revolution*. It was a collection of scripts from *The Horse Show Minute*, my weekday radio program. I had worked very hard on these short pieces and I felt they had a lot to offer. Plus, they worked as well in printed form as they did on the radio.

Lyons Press agreed and in 2005, we also released *Horse Smarts for the Busy Rider—Insights in Small Bites from* The Horse Show Minute *Radio Program*. Linda Parelli wrote the foreword. With more than 300 short pieces in eight categories, this book offers an easy way for any reader to develop a sense about horses.

As one gets older, thoughts of mortality are inevitable. There is something timeless about a book. In addition to the good it can serve during one's lifetime, it becomes a legacy, tangible evidence of your time on the planet. If you're really lucky, as I was, you get to preserve something that might have been lost.

Insights

- The principles underlying natural horsemanship go back more than 2,000 years.

- There have always been horsemen who sought to understand the horse's nature and communicate with him in ways he instinctively understood.

TRY THIS

Read Xenophon

There is one book I consider to be required reading for every aspiring horseman: *The Art of Horsemanship*. The author is Xenophon (430–355 B.C.), a Greek general, statesman, philosopher, writer, and horseman. This small book is a treatise he wrote in 360 B.C. for the rank and file cavalry soldiers in his command. It is the oldest complete text available today on empathetic, psychological horse training. Although it is more than 2,300 years old, it is an important reminder that the principles of good horsemanship are not new.

20 **The Riding Clinic**
Swallowing My Pride

My journey from human to Horseman has been marked by periods of slow but steady progress, periods of near stagnation, and periods of dramatic growth. One of those growth spurts occurred between 2003 and 2006, a time when I served as official emcee of Clinton Anderson's Walkabout Tour.

The Tour

The Walkabout Tour was a nationwide series of weekend seminars that taught horsemanship through demonstrations of Clinton working with young and problem horses. Crowds grew from a few hundred in the early years to 2,000 or more per event, due largely to Clinton's popular television program, *Downunder Horsemanship*®, on RFD-TV.

> People sometimes thought that I was the boss and Clinton worked for me. We got a good laugh out of that.

I accepted several responsibilities on the tour. First, I used my background in audio to assemble a portable sound system that dramatically improved the experience for audiences in the various venues where we performed.

The audio work was mostly behind the scenes. What the audience saw was that I was the official emcee and Clinton's sidekick. Apparently I did this with an air of confidence and authority, because people sometimes thought I was the boss and Clinton worked for me. We got a good laugh out of that.

I also did some teaching of my own at these events. Initially, it took the form of a trivia game I played with the audience before each of Clinton's segments. The questions were all true and false, or multiple choice. Sometimes, the correct answer was obvious, and I played it for laughs. Still, these questions gave me a jumping-off point for follow-up questions or to simply offer additional commentary on the subject. Most of the questions were on subjects that Clinton didn't cover: medical, breeds, history, and so on. If a member of the audience answered correctly, he or she won a prize, usually a plastic Downunder Horsemanship water bottle. "Yes, ladies and gentlemen," I would intone, "this is the very water bottle that Clinton himself uses!" That was guaranteed to get a laugh.

> Clinton encouraged people to ask me questions, saying that no one knew his methods better than me.

For my last two years on the tour, I also gave a half-hour talk after lunch on Sunday about the revolution in horsemanship and recounted some stories of great horsemen of the past, leading right up to Clinton, who I said then and still believe is one of the best teachers of horsemanship to ever come down the pike.

The more I taught, the more I learned, and the more people treated me like a horse expert. Clinton was partially responsible for this, as he invited people to bring their questions to me, saying that no one knew his methods better than me. That was probably true. Clinton and I were the only two people who had done all of his tour stops, about sixty of them by the time I left the tour, and through repeated exposure I absorbed a tremendous amount. I took his trust very seriously and made certain that I answered each question as he would. If I gave my own thoughts, I made that perfectly clear.

Clinics

In addition to his tour stops, Clinton also conducted riding clinics around the country. A clinic was for twenty riders and their horses. Seating was also provided for people who just wanted to watch or "audit" the clinic.

Clinton invited me repeatedly to ride in one of his clinics as his guest. Finally, in 2004, I accepted and immediately began stressing over it. If there was one thing I knew about Clinton, it was that he would expect me to expand my comfort zone. I was ready for that but I had one problem to lick first: I had never cantered Candy the way I used to canter Thunder.

The cattle drive helped me get over my general fear of riding, but I did not canter Trouble. The last time I'd cantered was when I fell off Thunder and was hurt so badly. I knew it was my own fault but that didn't prevent a phobia about cantering from developing. I wanted very much to get past it, but I couldn't do it alone. I needed help and I needed it before I went to Clinton's riding clinic, where everyone would know who I was and expect me to be a good rider.

I needed help and I needed it before I went to Clinton's riding clinic.

I turned to Karen Scholl. By this time, Karen had left the Parelli organization and was busy getting her career as an independent clinician off the ground. Diana and I had brainstormed with her about ways we could help each other; she would help us with our horses and we would help her through our radio program and recording studio. Already, she had worked with Diana and Savannah, and had helped me improve my groundwork with Sarah. With Karen, I could never be embarrassed or self-conscious. She had known me too long and was too easygoing to boot. We agreed to meet at Horse Lover's Park to work on my canter.

I showed up with all the *accoutrements* of the natural horseman: the nice horse, the Wade tree saddle with bucking rolls, the coiled lariat, the snaffle bit with rope reins and mecate, the chaps and the cowboy hat. In short, I looked the part, but I felt like a fraud. Karen didn't seem to notice. We worked for about an hour and in that time we got Candy cantering pretty well. Since I had only cantered her for a few strides at a time before, she had come to the conclusion that she didn't really need to canter with me and so there was always a little threat of a buck in her when I asked for the canter. You can imagine how I felt about that. That afternoon, we got through all of that and got me ready for the clinic.

I looked the part, but I felt like a fraud.

At least I *thought* I was ready. As it turned out, something I never dreamed would happen did. And it proved to be one of the most embarrassing moments of my life.

Insights

- The only way to get better at cantering is to do it.
- A horse that is not cantered regularly may show some resentment and negative behavior when asked.

TRY THIS

Get a Horse to Canter

One way to get a horse cantering after a long period of not being asked to do so is what Karen Scholl did with me. She started by working with Candy alone. Karen cantered her own horse and pulled Candy along behind. This is known as "ponying" the horse. The idea is to get the two horses cantering together. Then I climbed on and we repeated the exercise in a follow-the-leader fashion. Using another horse to get your horse cantering makes herd instinct work for you rather than against you.

21 The Cinch
Learning from Mistakes

Morning sessions in Clinton's riding clinics are devoted to groundwork and afternoon sessions are for riding. The first morning, Candy and I did really well on the groundwork. On the lunch break, I saddled her the way I always did and showed up at the arena ready to ride at the appointed hour.

Class began and Clinton reminded us all to be sure our girths were tight. We mounted up and started a series of riding exercises at the walk and the trot. I knew the canter was coming and felt I was ready for it.

Cruising

Clinton likes to have people do "cruising" lessons. That means riding around on a loose rein and not steering the horse at all. The horse can go anywhere he wants as long as he does not change gait. If it's a cruising lesson at the trot, he has to continue trotting anywhere he wants until you tell him to stop. With twenty riders all doing the cruising lesson in the same arena, there were plenty of near-wrecks. But the funny thing with horses is that if you leave them alone, they do just fine. Horses don't need our direction to avoid running into one another.

Horses don't need our direction to avoid running into one another.

Finally, Clinton upped the ante. It was time to canter but rather than having everyone cantering at once, Clinton had us go four or five at a time, while the rest of the riders sat on their horses in the arena, forming obstacles for our horses to maneuver around.

When my turn came, I leaned forward, kissed to Candy, and gave her a firm squeeze with my calves. She moved out nicely, a little faster than I wanted, but we were doing fine, cantering on a big loose rein. Clinton instructed me to grip the horn with my left hand and the back of my saddle with my right. I did as I was told and I felt even more secure.

We were cantering at a good clip toward the end of the arena and straight toward some standing horses. I was ready for Candy to go to the right but at the last moment she cut to the left instead. It threw me hard into the right stirrup and to my horror, my saddle slid to the right with me. Trying to pull myself back onto Candy's back only made the problem worse. Fortunately, Candy stopped almost immediately and I continued my slide to the right. When I was convinced I couldn't get back up, I let go and dropped to the ground, unhurt but embarrassed. Clinton was there in an instant and pushed the saddle back into place. A horse can go into a bucking frenzy in such situations, but Candy was solid as a rock. Clinton cinched the saddle tightly and I climbed back aboard to resume my cantering. I laughed it off but knew it would stand as one of the most humiliating moments of my life.

Candy cut to the left, throwing me hard into the right stirrup.

It was the kind of thing that just didn't happen to a really experienced rider. I'd been overly concerned about making Candy uncomfortable with a tight cinch. Since that day, I've taken Clinton's only slightly tongue-in-cheek advice to heart: "Pull the cinch so tight your horse's eyes roll back." I do it a bit at a time, of course. Just snug enough to hold the saddle in place at first. Then I walk the horse around a bit and maybe do a bit of lungeing. The cinch can usually be tightened considerably after that. The third time comes after I've been riding for five minutes or so.

If I need to tighten the cinch a fourth or fifth time, I do.

If I need to tighten the cinch a fourth or fifth time, I do. If the saddle has a rear cinch, I make that snug. A breast collar helps hold the saddle in place, too, and I never ride without one of those now.

The rest of my clinic experience was excellent. As I suspected he would, Clinton packed an incredible amount of information and hands-on experience into those three days. About the middle of the next week I was still high from it—and had not thought about the cinch incident for some time—when I received an email from a woman I did not know.

Criticism

I've been lucky, I suppose. I've had very few pot shots taken at me during my ten years in the horse industry. I'm out there. I'm visible. Some would say I'm successful at what I do and I'm sure many people think I have a pretty great life. I do, but it's no accident. I've earned it with hard work, making sacrifices, and taking chances. Still, some people, for reasons I will never understand, think they need to tear down those who succeed as though that success is taking something away from them. Such was the woman who wrote me this email.

> Some people think they need to tear down those who succeed.

She explained that she was one of several women from her barn who had audited Clinton's riding clinic the previous weekend, meaning they had sat in the stands and watched instead of taking part in the actual clinic. She had been voted the one to write to express their feelings. They had expected me to be a much better rider, she said, and were shocked that I would have the problem with my cinch after Clinton had specifically warned us about that. Furthermore, she criticized my horse, claiming that Candy was undernourished, needed to be fed beet pulp, and was too young to be ridden in the clinic. As Candy was eight years old at the time and in full flesh, those comments were absurd. I realized later that she might have read somewhere that I had a two-year-old filly and thought I had brought Sarah to the riding clinic instead of Candy. That the writer and her friends couldn't tell the difference between a two-year-old filly and an eight-year-old mare was illuminating, to say the least.

> That the writer couldn't tell the difference between a two-year-old filly and an eight-year-old mare was illuminating.

Still, the email hurt. It was exactly the sort of thing I was afraid would happen. I had made it my policy to always answer emails, but this one I considered ignoring. Finally, I wrote her back and told her that I had come to the clinic to learn from Clinton just like everyone else and that I made no apologies for my horse or me. There was no response.

In the months that followed, I would occasionally run into people who were at that clinic and they would sometimes rib me about tightening my cinch. I didn't mind because those people did it to my face and were not malicious about it. It was just their way of engaging me in conversation. I no longer worry about that sort of thing. I even ride on television for the whole world to see. I receive validation every single day from my readers, listeners, and viewers that they are educated and entertained by what I do, and that they find value in my efforts. They accept me for who I am and that gives me the confidence to continue on my own journey, both in private and in public.

Insights

- To make progress at anything, you must take chances.
- There will always be petty people who criticize those trying to better themselves.
- A cinch should be tightened multiple times.
- A breast collar will prevent a saddle from sliding off to one side.

TRY THIS

Tightening the Cinch

Take a deep breath from the diaphragm and notice how your waistline expands. If you tightened your belt at this time, it would be loose when you exhaled and went back to normal breathing. This is what a horse does when you tighten the cinch of a saddle. He bloats himself up. My cousins' pony, Fury, did this every time he was saddled, so my Uncle John routinely kneed him in the belly to get him to exhale. That little trick got the job done but contributed to Fury's sour attitude about being ridden. Tightening the cinch in stages is far better.

22 | **Lessons in Trust**
Expecting the Best from a Horse

Diana has lived in England and Canada, in addition to the United States. Our kids have traveled in Central America, South America, Europe, and Asia since leaving the nest. But until January of 2006, I'd never spent time outside the United States. That's when Diana and I spent ten incredible days in Brazil (Photo 20).

Going International

The occasion was the First International Equus Congress, an event organized by a young Brazilian equine veterinarian named Dr. Fernando Rolim. Clinicians and veterinarians from five countries converged to give presentations on natural horsemanship and mulemanship, and to see some of the top breeding operations in Brazil. Dr. Robert M. Miller was the headliner of the event. I was the emcee.

There were many things about the trip that were memorable—the lush rolling landscape, the stunning horses, mules, and donkeys, the extravagant barns and riding arenas, the luxurious homes, the fine food, the fellowship with the other presenters, and the warmth and hospitality of the Brazilian people we met—but one thing always comes to my mind now when I think about how this trip affected my journey: in Brazil, I learned an important lesson about the power of trust.

An offering of trust is an offering of vulnerability.

Think about the notion of trust for a moment. Trust cannot be purchased; it can't be taken, it can only be offered willingly and accepted graciously. An offering of trust is an offering of vulnerability. When you trust someone, you put yourself at his mercy. You place your faith in that person and visualize him doing the right thing by you.

Language Barrier

The proprietor of our host ranch, Criatório Campeãs da Gameleira, was Martin Herman. A successful bioengineer, he spoke several languages, but English was not one of them. Still, he tried gamely throughout our visit to communicate with us in our native tongue. It was a terrific struggle for him, and I admired him for making the effort. He put himself out there. He trusted that we would not become impatient with him or mock his efforts. And we didn't. Eventually, I discovered that he spoke German and I worked up the courage to attempt a conversation with him using the German I remembered from high school and college. In doing so, I had to trust him the same way he trusted the rest of us. I could tell he really appreciated my doing so.

A Stallion in the Dark

Another experience where the theme of trust surfaced took place one evening when a group of us were viewing Herman's fine horses, mules, and donkeys in a grassy paddock at the center of the barn complex. One of the horses, a white Mangalarga Marchador stallion, was saddled and offered to any of us who wanted to try him. The Mangalarga Marchador is the national horse of Brazil and is an even-tempered, versatile gaited horse that is starting to catch on here in the States.

The only sound was the even cadence of the stallion's steel shoes on the gravel beneath us.

At the time, however, I knew nothing about these horses. After a couple of other people in our party had ridden him briefly, I decided to take a ride. I had very little experience with gaited horses at the time, and I had never ridden a stallion.

I pointed the horse down the gravel road toward our cottages, picked up the reins to make contact with his mouth and squeezed my calves.

He moved into a nicely collected four-beat gait akin to a running walk or amble. I had intended to ride a hundred yards or so before turning around. But in seconds, the lights of the viewing area disappeared behind us and we had nothing but moonlight peeking through the trees on either side of the road to light the way. The only sound was the even cadence of the stallion's steel shoes on the gravel beneath us.

I was nervous, but I chose to relax and give myself totally to this marvelous experience. In other words, I gave the horse my trust. He did not abuse it. We rode on through the darkness and reached the area of the guest cottages, turned around and came back to the paddock. The ride lasted probably no more than fifteen minutes but it was exhilarating nonetheless.

Oscar Performance

My greatest lesson involving trust, however, occurred on the final day of demonstrations, and it took a while for its significance to sink in.

One of the presenters at the event was a fifty-seven-year-old horse trainer from Argentina named Oscar Scarpati Schmid. The rest of us knew nothing about him. He spoke only Spanish and didn't hang out with the rest of us. In spite of the language barrier, I could see that he had a certain charisma, a brightness and joy about him. He seemed to attract people to him.

Tanned and bearded, with curly salt-and-pepper hair, Oscar wore canvas slippers over his bare feet, roomy, khaki pants and a loose-fitting, long-sleeve shirt. In a sea of Wrangler blue denim jeans, starched Western shirts, cowboy hats, and boots, Oscar stood out dramatically. He looked more like a college professor or Hollywood film director than a horse trainer.

During the opening ceremonies he gave the audience a taste of what was to come, but it went over my head, as I had other things on my mind at the time. It was not until the end of our final day, when Oscar worked with a young horse in the round pen that his horsemanship got my full attention.

First, he removed the slippers. Barefoot and empty-handed, he approached the large bay Lusitano mare. Suddenly he crouched and charged head-on, waving his arms like a madman, and darting left and right. As the mare began to panic he collapsed in the sand at her feet and quietly caressed her front legs. She quickly stopped moving.

Rising slowly, Oscar moved to the horse's midsection where he draped himself over her topline, slipped a leg under her belly, and began stroking her far gaskin with his bare foot. Then it was the near gaskin. When she moved, he let her carry him, his bare feet dangling inches from heavy hooves. One moment he was hanging from her neck, walking his feet up her chest and putting her neck in an inverted leg lock. The next moment, he was standing on her back. The next, he was crawling under the mare, picking up her feet and placing them on his head or in his mouth. Through all of this, she seemed as baffled as we did. But she was calm and did not hurt him. He was soon riding her bareback and bridleless about the round pen.

> He was crawling under the mare, picking up her feet and placing them on his head or in his mouth.

Oscar spoke in Spanish and his words were translated into Portuguese and English by fellow Argentinean, Michele Hahn, a Monty Roberts-certified natural horsemanship instructor who was also a presenter at the event. He explained that his mentor, a native of the Pampas named Don Cristóbal Luna, taught him this traditional Indian method of mimicking the behavior of a superior horse in a herd. Someone whispered to me that Oscar had autism and thus connected in a special way with animals. If so, his was a strange form of autism, for it lived side by side with the flamboyance and bravado of a circus performer.

Pressed by the media for his reaction to Oscar's performance, Dr. Miller spoke for us all. "I can't explain what I just saw," he said. "I'll be thinking about it for the next year."

Taking Chances

There was a lesson for me in Oscar's demonstration, I felt certain. As we were leaving the arena that day, I caught up with Michele Hahn and asked what she made of it. She spoke of Oscar's childlike innocence keeping him safe from injury. Maybe the lesson was about trust, I thought. About the need to give trust in order to get it.

I've been experimenting with this idea, that I must take a chance on the horse just as I ask him to take a chance on me. Trust, like respect, is a two-way street. If I want both the horse's respect and his trust, I must be willing to give the same. But who goes first? Must I, in the name of my own self-preservation, wait to offer my trust until I'm certain that there is no danger for me in doing so? If that is the case, then I am expecting a lot of the horse, for this creature has a self-preservation instinct, too, one that is just as powerful as my own.

> I can offer my trust to the horse while remaining alert and ready to act.

Perhaps the answer lies in striking a proper balance. I can offer my trust to the horse while remaining alert and ready to act should my safety be threatened. This is part of being mentally engaged and focused on what you're doing when you're working with a horse. I have the feeling that Oscar, even as he lay on the ground with his face between the hind feet of the horse, or when he placed his teeth on a hoof, was very tuned in to the horse's body language and was ready to do whatever was necessary to save himself if something went awry. But nothing went awry, and maybe the reason it didn't was because he trusted the horse. He said through his behavior, "I know you can hurt me or take advantage of me, but I don't believe you will."

I will close this chapter on trust with what might seem like an odd analogy: marriage and the prenuptial agreement. I know why people have prenuptial agreements and I used to think it was just being smart, a way of protecting your assets should a relationship turn sour. I now see it differently. I see it as a sign that you don't really trust the person you are marrying. Or perhaps you don't trust yourself to remain faithful and give your all to the relationship. It may very well be a self-fulfilling prophecy, something that becomes inevitable because you have planned for it.

Human relationships and horse relationships have so many things in common. This is simply another example. Trust, freely given and graciously accepted, enriches both.

Insights

- Trust requires vulnerability.

- People and animals may rise to become worthy of the trust we offer them.

- Trusting does not require abandoning your own self-preservation.

TRY THIS

Offer Trust

Rather than being tensed up and on guard continually around your horse, try trusting him. *Expect* him to be a gentleman and chances are very good that he will be just that. Trusting your horse doesn't mean being stupid, however. Remain alert but place a clear expectation in your brain that your horse is worthy of your trust.

23 The Rearing Horse
The How and Why of Laying a Horse Down

One of the key insights that came out of writing my book with Dr. Miller was that to become an effective leader with a horse, you must show him, in ways he instinctively understands, that you can control his movement.

Controlling Movement

A horse's movement can be controlled in three ways: it can be caused, it can be changed, and it can be inhibited. From the earliest days of my journey, I routinely saw examples of causing and changing movement. Round pen training, groundwork exercises done on a lead line, and riding make extensive use of them. They can be very effective.

But it wasn't until I began researching horsemanship of the past that I came to understand the importance of inhibiting movement. Especially in the 1800s, inhibiting a horse's movement by "laying him down" was a common way of taming wild horses or dealing with problem horses.

Modern readers became aware of this procedure in the 1995 best-selling book *The Horse Whisperer* by Nicholas Evans. It was performed by the main character, Tom Booker, as a way of finally breaking through to the troubled horse, Pilgrim. Readers of that book were also introduced to John Solomon Rarey (1827–1866), the real-life Ohio horseman who perfected laying down a horse. Rarey is one of my favorite historical

> Ohio horseman, John Solomon Rarey, perfected laying down a horse.

characters. I wrote about him in *The Revolution in Horsemanship*, in a column for *Horse & Rider* magazine, and in a television segment.

But those were all words and pictures. The power of laying a horse down came alive for me in Waterloo, Iowa, in 2006. It was a Clinton Anderson tour stop and like all of them, this one featured a young horse for Clinton to start under saddle and two other so-called problem horses. One of these was for the trailer-loading demo and the other was for the de-spooking demo. It was the spooky horse that I will always remember.

It was a light buckskin Quarter Horse gelding, stocky, nice-looking, and freshly groomed. The owner brought the horse out and, as was usually the case in such demos, she had no idea how to control him. Conse-

More than once I had to thump a horse on the forehead with Clinton's expensive German microphone.

quently, he was all over the place, crowding into her repeatedly as if she were not there. One of my little jobs on the tour was to walk out with each owner and hold the microphone up to her mouth when Clinton interviewed her about her horse. Unfortunately, that always put me in the same danger as the owner. More than once I had to thump a horse on the forehead with Clinton's expensive German microphone to keep the horse from running over me. Finally I began simply handing the microphone to the owner and stepping back. That's what I did in this case.

Clinton talked with the woman about her horse for several minutes while the horse danced around her. I sometimes suspected that Clinton prolonged these little interviews for dramatic effect. You always wondered if the owner would escape unscathed, and of course, the more you saw of the horse's bad behavior, the more impressed you were when Clinton turned the horse around. In this case, he would effect an incredible transformation, just as he had with the other 200-plus horses I'd seen him train, but he would do it in a very different way.

Classic Horse Taming at Work

When Clinton finally took the lead rope from the owner, the audience gave a collective sigh of relief and politely applauded her. Although she was probably responsible for the horse's current state, she had been brave enough to bring the horse out.

As he always did, Clinton immediately backed the horse out of his space by adopting an assertive posture, jerking hard on the lead rope and waving his training stick aggressively in the gelding's face. That worked initially, but as he started lungeing the horse and getting control of its front and back end, the horse began rearing.

When a horse first rears, it is usually an honest expression of his survival instinct, an attempt to gain relief from whatever pressure the handler is applying. If the handler rewards this behavior by removing the pressure, the horse learns to rear in such situations. Rearing changes from being motivated by survival to being motivated by disrespect and laziness. That's what had happened with the buckskin gelding.

> Rearing changes from being motivated by survival to being motivated by disrespect and laziness.

Clinton followed his own advice for handling rearing horses and simply let the taut lead rope play out a bit. In doing so he could keep pressure on the horse from a safe distance. The reasoning is that the horse can't stay up there for very long because it takes too much effort. When the horse comes down, the pressure can be taken away as a reward for returning to terra firma. The problem usually goes away when the horse becomes convinced that rearing doesn't buy him anything.

This horse, however, continued to rear, no matter what Clinton did. In fact, the rearing seemed to get worse, more frequent and more aggressive, with plenty of pawing at the rope. I stood at the edge of the arena and watched an amazing demonstration of classic horse taming unfold.

One thing that experience does for you is it gives you more options. Clinton's experience told him it was time to do something different. He gave the horse a short reprieve while he acquired a 45-foot lariat rope from his apprentice and formed a small loop with one end. Approaching the horse casually, Clinton gave it a good rub with the rope. Then he picked up the left front foot as though he were going to clean it out, but instead slipped the loop over it. The horse didn't seem to mind. Slowly but deliberately, Clinton ran the free end of the rope over the horse's back and under its belly, creating a makeshift surcingle. Then he stepped back and played the rope out.

> The horse began hopping about on three legs, shaking his head and trying to free the tied leg.

For a few moments, the horse did not realize the predicament he was in. He had one leg tied up and a rope around his belly. When he understood, he immediately began hopping about on three legs, shaking his head and trying to free the tied leg. Clinton simply followed him from a distance, keeping the long rope taut and out of the horse's way.

At last, the horse came to a stop, obviously tired and uncertain about what was going on. Then Clinton began pulling lightly on the rope. The horse resisted for a while, but eventually took a hopping step to get some relief from the pulling. Clinton removed the pressure momentarily, then began pulling again. This time, instead of hopping, the horse went down on the flexed knee, but came right back up. Clinton pulled again and the horse went down again, but this time it stayed in this awkward position, its hindquarters in the air, its right front leg extended, and most of its weight on the knee of the flexed left leg.

> **The horse made the choice to lie down.**

Clinton held its position but made no effort to pull the horse down. In less than a minute, the horse slowly rolled onto its side.

After the Horse Is Down

What struck me about the demonstration was that Clinton had not forced the horse to do anything. He had simply orchestrated the situation in such a way that the right thing—lying down—was easy to do, and the wrong thing—remaining on its feet—was difficult. The horse made the choice to lie down of its own free will.

> **The horse lay perfectly still, a very different animal than a few minutes earlier.**

Once the horse was stretched out on its side, Clinton approached it carefully and began rubbing its body, its neck, and its head. After a minute or so of this, he casually loosened the rope and straightened the flexed leg. Then he removed the rope entirely and continued rubbing the horse. The horse lay perfectly still, a very different animal from the one that, a few minutes earlier, had been rearing and pawing.

Clinton had talked little during this procedure, which in itself added to the drama. At this point I asked Clinton if I could make a few comments to the audience while he continued. He happily agreed. I drew upon what I had learned from working on *The Revolution in Horsemanship*. I pointed out that for a prey animal whose survival depends upon being able to take flight and outrun predators, lying down is the ultimate act of submission. It places the horse in the most vulnerable of all positions and proves, beyond any shadow of a doubt, that the creature that causes it is dominant.

> In the horse's mind, he doesn't lie down in the presence of a predator unless he is about to die.

Laying a horse down is an extreme form of controlling movement and the horse responds with an extreme form of submission. In the horse's mind, he doesn't lie down in the presence of a predator unless he is about to die. Nature has given him the ability to mentally check out at that moment. A zebra downed by a lion will struggle until he is flat on his side, then do the same thing. He submits, completely and unconditionally. It's a way, experts speculate, of sparing the brain the horror of imminent, brutal death.

All the time I was talking, Clinton was rubbing and comforting the prostrate horse. When I had finished, Clinton began urging the horse to its feet. This is sometimes the hardest part. Finally, the horse rose and shook the dirt from its coat. It stood with its head lowered and a hind foot cocked. Occasionally it licked its lips or made a chewing motion with its mouth. Clinton began working with the horse again on its

> Teaching a trained horse to lie down upon cue is a trust-building exercise

groundwork. This time the horse was respectful and responsive, with no sign that it wanted to rear. The spooky object demo continued but I really don't remember much more than that. The ballet of horsemanship I had just seen was consuming my thoughts.

John Rarey often laid the horse down multiple times, getting it to the point that it willingly laid down with a simple cue. Many horsemen today have taught their trained horses to lie down upon cue. It is a trust-building exercise, a way of tuning up the horse's mind, as Ray Hunt puts it. It's a valuable thing to teach a horse, a neat trick to show your friends, and a reminder that you will never take advantage of the horse when it is at its most vulnerable.

Throwing a Horse

Historically, another term was often used for laying a horse down: *throwing* the horse. While throwing was intended to get the horse flat on the ground and produce the same end result—a horse that is calm, respectful, and compliant—the word itself has a different connotation than laying the horse down. It connotes a physical battle. More force was involved and there wasn't as much waiting on the horse. The horse could hit the ground hard and in a panic. He could hurt himself or those around him.

Laying a horse down is not for beginners.

Like many other nineteenth-century horsemen, Captain Matthew Horace Hayes, a prominent British veterinarian and author, practiced throwing as a way of gentling horses. But he came to decry the practice as being too dangerous. His change of heart came from an incident that took place in Africa in which he threw a horse and its back was broken.

Laying a horse down is not for beginners. Even professional horse trainers need to take great care in learning the method and using it. It is a powerful tool but like many things, that power can also make it dangerous.

Insights

- Extreme measures are sometimes necessary to reach a horse with extreme problems.

- Laying a horse down is another means of controlling his movement.

- Horsemen of the past are worth studying.

TRY THIS

Learn to Lay a Horse Down

Most people don't have the skills, desire, or need to lay a horse down. However, if you have all three, I recommend starting with a gentle, well-trained horse before trying it with a problem horse. Clinton Anderson, Ken McNabb, and other clinicians have excellent videos that show in a step-by-step way how it is done. Study one of these methods thoroughly and approach this matter with a great deal of forethought.

24 **A Bit of Pressure**
Giving a Rogue Horse a New Start

A few weeks after Waterloo, Clinton's tour came to the fairgrounds in Puyallup, Washington. It was a venue I knew well, having appeared there several times at a horse expo called Equimasters. This 2006 tour stop would become my dominant memory of the facility.

Faster than the Eye

For one thing, Clinton arranged a special treat for the large audience. Our good friend, Ted Blocker, who was on the tour to promote his Tie Ring, demonstrated his fast draw talents. Both Ted and his wife, Jean, had been champion fast draw artists in days past. The speed with which Ted could draw a Colt 45 single-action revolver from a holster and fire it was stunning.

Both of Ted's pistols were loaded with blanks, much like those used in cowboy mounted shooting. In the middle of the arena, in front of nearly 2,000 people, Ted handed Clinton one of the loaded pistols and made sure it was aimed at the ground.

"Cock the hammer," he instructed, "and when you see me start to draw, pull the trigger."

The implication was that Ted could draw his gun from its holster, cock the hammer and fire it more quickly than Clinton could simply pull his trigger. At this time Clinton was about thirty years old and Ted was in his mid-sixties.

"Are you ready, Clinton?" Ted asked.

"Go for it, mate," Clinton replied.

Bam ... bam! Faster than the eye could see, Ted had drawn and fired his gun. Clinton's shot was half a second behind.

Clinton was shocked. "Let's do that again," he demanded.

"Sure. Ready?" Ted said.

Clinton watched Ted's hand intently. "Ready."

Bam ... bam! Again, Clinton was late. The simple fact was that Ted drew and fired faster than the image could register in Clinton's brain and send an impulse to his trigger finger. Ted is a person of many talents who gets more interesting to me all the time.

A Doomed Horse

Later that same afternoon, Ted and I stood together at the edge of the arena and watched Clinton do his trailer-loading demo. We had heard about this horse. Refusing to go into a trailer was really the least of his problems. The horse, a stout, 1,200-pound bay Quarter Horse, was owned by a slender, delicate woman with a speech impediment and some physical problems, the extent of which I couldn't really judge. There was goodness and intelligence in her eyes and I gave her a lot of credit for stepping into that arena in front of all those people and telling her story. The pairing of this human with this horse was one of the worst mismatches I had ever seen, yet she loved the horse and refused to give up on him.

> The pairing of this human with this horse was one of the worst mismatches I had ever seen.

The horse, it seemed, not only refused to enter a trailer, it fought her and tried to get away when she attempted to lead it. Twice already that weekend, the horse had broken away, once from her and once from Clinton's apprentice, and run loose on the fairgrounds. The horse was so strong and so defiant that Clinton's standard rope halter, which had enough of a bite to it to discourage most horses from pulling against it, meant nothing. Upon hearing of the difficulties in controlling this horse, Clinton had ordered it put in a snaffle bit instead of a rope halter. The bit would give him greater control than the rope halter. I hadn't known him do that before. That alone told me this would be worth seeing.

Clinton began working with the horse as it always did, backing it out of his space and asking it to lunge around him. The horse gave a half-hearted try then nearly yanked Clinton off his feet. Putting on some gloves, Clinton steeled himself for what he knew was going to be a real fight. Little did he know that the fight would continue long after he had finished working with the horse.

> Little did Clinton know that the fight would continue long after he had finished working with the horse.

For at least forty-five minutes, Clinton did battle with this horse, insisting that it respect his space and move its feet in response to his commands. The horse resisted at every turn, but at every turn, Clinton was ready for it. Frankly, Clinton had to become very aggressive with this horse, yanking on its mouth and spanking it hard with his training stick. Anyone who came into this in the middle would surely think Clinton was abusing this horse. Occasionally, there were flashes of anger on Clinton's part, but time and again I saw him rein in his emotions and return to a business-like attitude.

Finally, the horse started coming around and I saw Clinton's attitude lighten. With superb restraint, he continued to ply the horse with groundwork until it would stand in one place, head low, and body relaxed, licking and chewing. It was very nearly as impressive as what I had seen in Waterloo. The trailer-loading demo then continued without incident.

> With superb restraint, he continued to ply the horse with groundwork.

The licking and chewing action is always a positive sign to a horse trainer. When a horse is worried or fearful or aggressive, his jaw is clamped shut. When he is taking flight or thinking about taking flight, the mouth is closed and his nasal airway—the only way a horse takes in air—is open wide. Licking and chewing thus means the jaw is no longer clenched and the horse is not thinking flight. Some trainers see licking and chewing as a sign of submission. Monty Roberts says it's as if the horse is saying, "I'm just a harmless grazing animal; you can be leader of our team." Mike Kevil believes it is simply a natural result of relaxing a part of the body that had been tensed. If you had clenched your fist and then relaxed it, you might wiggle your fingers a bit. Clinton sees it as a sign the horse is thinking about the lesson, that he is, "licking the dust off his brain." Regardless of the exact meaning, trainers are always pleased to see this bit of body language coming from a horse.

Emotion Takes Over

Sitting at my booth a bit later, I was approached by a pleasant-looking young woman who introduced herself and complimented me on my book with Dr. Miller. She was actively involved in natural horsemanship, she said with pride, and moderated an online chat room on that subject. She

That horse had three feet in the grave.

went on to say that she was impressed with what Clinton had accomplished with the trailer-loading horse, but was also a bit disappointed. I asked why and she said that she felt he had misread the horse. She then gave her analysis of the horse's personality type and explained how such horses should be handled.

I listened politely but felt that the woman did not appreciate the extreme nature of the horse's behavior. I had been in the arena near that horse while Clinton interviewed the owner. The fact is, that horse had three feet in the grave. Horses that dangerous are usually sent to slaughter. On that day, Clinton had saved the horse's life. He met the horse's aggression with aggression of his own. That was the degree of firmness that was necessary. When the session was over, the horse was calm and respectful. It had a chance to go on living, to be the sort of horse someone would want to own. If the owner made a similar change and became an effective leader to that horse, their life together would be dramatically different.

I could not fault Clinton on anything I saw. In fact, I was very proud of him for being willing to do that in front of an audience, knowing full well that there would be people, such as this woman, who did not understand what they saw and would criticize him.

A week or so later I received a lengthy email from the same woman. It included pictures of her horse and more flowery, seemingly heartfelt praise of *The Revolution in Horsemanship*. I replied briefly to thank her.

A few days later, I received another email from her. This one had a very different tone. She chastised Clinton for his handling of the trailer-loading horse and me for being associated with him. I thought carefully about my reply, knowing that it would soon be coursing across the

Internet. I replied that Clinton did what was necessary to turn around a very dangerous horse, one that was certainly destined for the slaughterhouse if something dramatic did not happen to change its behavior. I also commented that every good horseman—even the one she followed so loyally—would do the same thing in private. I considered it courageous that Clinton did it in public where all of us could watch and learn.

I could feel the situation starting to unravel.

I received no reply directly from this woman, but a bit later a different woman contacted me. She was at the Puyallup event and had a very different take on Clinton's performance. She was also in the chat group that had been hashing all of this over. She just wanted me to know that my defense of Clinton had been blasted by the first woman, not to me but to others in her little online world. I could feel the situation starting to unravel.

A week later came the icing on the cake: I learned from Clinton's office that this woman had sent a letter critical of Clinton to each of his sponsors, trying to damage those relationships and affect Clinton's career. Fortunately, Clinton's sponsors did not overreact. With the number of people Clinton reaches through his television program, video products, and public appearances, it was completely understandable that he would rub someone the wrong way.

Never underestimate the emotion some people have about horses.

The lesson I learned from this is to never underestimate the emotion some people have about horses. This woman had good intentions but at her place on her journey, she simply didn't understand what she saw. Instead of driving her to reflection, her emotions drove her to action. Something told me that one day this woman would look back and see this incident with different eyes.

I was right. About a year later, I got another email from the same woman. This time she praised Clinton for something she had seen him do more recently. Why she sent it to me I don't know. Maybe she wanted me to know that she was making progress on her journey. I was tempted to write back and ask her if she had expressed these new feelings of hers to Clinton's sponsors, as well, but I resisted the urge.

Insights

- Lack of experience can cause people to misinterpret what they see.
- An aggressive horse must be dealt with firmly.
- Anger and retribution have no place in handling horses.

TRY THIS

Be as Gentle as Possible

The next time you ask your horse to do something, be as subtle and gentle with the request as possible. Place in your mind a picture of the horse doing exactly what you want him to do and focus on that image. Next, raise the energy in your body to tell him it's time to pay attention. Then give the cue with the lightest touch possible. Be alert to any sort of try—even shifting his weight—and reward that try. If you get nothing, raise the intensity of the request the smallest amount you can and try again. By always starting gently and only becoming as firm as necessary to get an acceptable try, you will be teaching your horse to be become lighter and more responsive every day.

25 Learning from Lyons
Practical Perspectives from an Original

During the past ten years, I've made many good friends in the horse industry. I'm proud to say that one of them is John Lyons. John has a huge and loyal following, and has been recognized both inside and outside the industry for his skill as an educator. As far as I can tell, John has developed most of his thinking on horses and horsemanship on his own, without any real mentors. That's not good or bad. It's just different.

Making a Change

In a way, John and I have similar stories. John became obsessed with horses after a successful career as a salesman of orthopedic supplies in Kansas City. In his early thirties, he was making a six-figure income but left it all behind to become a Colorado rancher, something he knew almost nothing about.

> Through circumstances beyond his control, John's ranching career flopped.

Through circumstances beyond his control—an economic downturn and uncooperative weather—John's ranching career flopped. But in the process, he discovered that he had the ability to share what he was learning about horses and he didn't have to be the world's best horse trainer to get started helping people. John has come a long way since those early days and today he is, to hundreds of thousands of horse owners, "America's Most Trusted Horseman."

Not long after I met John, I pitched him the idea of doing a series of audio tapes to share some of his training ideas. I was convinced that audio is superior in some ways to video since it can be fully experienced while doing other activities: driving, exercising, working, etc. John agreed and we created a series of five tapes called *A Conversation with John Lyons*. These were face-to-face discussions between John and me on a variety of topics of importance to him. We recorded them in my studio over a period of two days in 1999. The content John shared in these tapes, which are now available in CD form, is superb.

John's concepts have helped me tremendously and I'd like to share some of them here.

Fear

If the truth were known, I think most people who have horses or ride regularly have had some fear issues related to horses at some time in their lives. Mine started with my fall from Thunder. Diana had a similar incident not long after we got our own horses. The first thing John taught me is that fear is normal. It is natural. And most importantly, it is healthy. "Fear is common sense in disguise. It's your survival instinct at work," John says.

"Fear is common sense in disguise."

What a marvelous gift he gives us! Instead of being ashamed of being frightened, you can actually celebrate your fear as a sure sign that your antenna is working. But fear can stop us from doing things we want to do, which is not good. If you want to change that, if you want to make your fear go away, John's method can help.

The secret is to do something. Anything! Action is your friend; inaction is your enemy. Fear comes from feeling you have no control, so you start where you feel you're in control and build from there. If you're afraid to even stand next to a horse, that's okay, but don't avoid him altogether. Instead, stand outside his stall and pet him through the bars. If you do that every day, you will become bored with it and want to do more. That's when you might enter the stall and groom the horse. When you get bored with that, you might halter the horse and lead him around the corral. Your comfort zone, while small in the beginning, naturally grows larger through activity. Continue this and you'll be able to regain the confidence you lost through the fear-producing incident.

It's important to recognize that John doesn't advise forcing yourself to confront your fear and conquer it through force of will. The approach he takes is comfortable and preserves what we all love about horses: they make us feel good when we're around them.

The Replacement Concept

The Replacement Concept is John's alternative to saying "No" to a horse. He simply gives the horse something positive to do that takes the place of the negative behavior. The underlying premise here is that horses can't think about two things at once, at least not the same way we humans can. "The horse has a one-track mind," is one way this is often phrased. I know there are people who dispute this, who claim that the horse can think of multiple things at once, but I simply don't believe it.

Horses can't think about two things at once.

Let's put this in human terms for a moment. Suppose you are driving home from work with some music playing on the radio and a coworker in the front seat beside you. Your brain is most likely handling several threads of thought simultaneously: it is driving the car, it is listening to the music, it is thinking about dinner, it is carrying on a conversation with your passenger, and taking in the sights outside. Now, it is possible, I agree, that these are really *concurrent* thoughts—that the brain is switching quickly between different thoughts much like a computer processor can have multiple programs running at the same time, as opposed to having several processors running separate programs simultaneously. This is splitting hairs. The point is that this is something humans take for granted that horses simply can't do.

For instance, if a horse is pawing and you want him to stop, John would say to give him a cue to do something else. Maybe you ask him to back up or move his hindquarters over or lower his head. When the horse turns his attention to executing the cue, he forgets about pawing.

Although I've never heard John say this in so many words, I think that keeping your thoughts positive makes it less likely that the horse will feel threatened. Reprimanding a horse is more likely to ignite his fear than asking him to do something else.

The Calm Down Cue

There is a special case of the Replacement Concept that is very handy. John calls it the Calm Down Cue. In a nutshell, it's a cue given through the bridle that replaces nervous energy with calmness. The cue causes the horse to lower his head all the way to the ground. If you have good timing and feel, you can teach this to any horse in a matter of fifteen minutes or less.

Why does lowering his head to the ground cause a horse to calm down? The answer, as usual, goes back to the horse's underlying nature. The horse is a grazer; he lowers his head to eat grass. But a horse will only do this when he feels safe, because lowering his head to the ground puts him out of position to instantly take flight. To take off running, he has to raise his head and throw his weight back onto his hindquarters, the source of all his power. Grazing puts his weight on his front end. The split second it takes to reposition himself from grazing to taking flight could be the difference between life and death for a prey animal.

> Lowering his head to the ground puts a horse out of position to instantly take flight.

A horse is therefore very careful about when he puts his head down. So if he lowers his head as a conditioned response to the human's cue, his brain plays a little trick on him. The mental dialogue would go something like this: "I never put my head down unless I'm safe. I'm putting my head down. Therefore, I must be safe." That produces a calming effect on the horse.

The Yes Answer Cue

If you apply pressure to a horse as a cue to perform in a certain way, you take away the pressure when he gives you a try. In the language of operant conditioning, this is known as negative reinforcement because something unpleasant is removed from the situation as a way of rewarding the horse and reinforcing the behavior. This works, but it works even bet-

ter when it is combined with positive reinforcement, something pleasant added to the equation. It might be a verbal, "Good boy!" It might be
an affectionate stroke on the neck or scratch on
the withers. It could even be a food treat of some
kind. John calls this a Yes Answer Cue.

Removing pressure works even better when it is combined with a positive reward.

The key is consistency. The cue must be the
same every time you use it. The horse learns that it is a good thing and
views it as a reward when it is used.

Getting Your Horse's Attention

John has a very interesting take on the relationship between getting a
horse's attention and getting him to perform in a certain way.

Most people would say that getting the horse's attention comes first,
that once he is paying attention to you, you can communicate your wishes
to him and he will perform accordingly. John teaches the exact opposite
regarding the horse's attention.

He starts by pointing out that we really have four factors at work here:
the horse's attention, the horse's performance, the trainer's attention, and
the trainer's performance. John contends that the progression in a training session really goes like this:

1 The trainer's attention
2 The trainer's performance
3 The horse's performance
4 The horse's attention

In other words, it all starts in the trainer's mind, when he directs
his attention to what he wants to accomplish. That is translated into a
physical act performed by the trainer, a cue given to
the horse, pressure applied and released. Next comes
the horse's physical response to the cue or pressure, in

Attention is a byproduct of respect.

other words, the horse's performance. The end result is that the horse
gives his attention to the trainer.

Attention is a byproduct of respect. This goes back again to the notion of controlling a horse's movement as a way of reaching his mind and establishing your right to lead the team. When you prove to the horse that you can control his movement, the horse sees you as leader, he gives you his respect and his attention. You can't simply demand that. It comes from action.

The Lesson Plan

John advocates careful planning of any training done with a horse. The model he uses is the teacher and the student. A good teacher has a lesson plan. So does a good horse trainer. There are enough steps in the lesson plan to make it easy for the horse to do. If a horse has trouble with any of the steps, John says to simply break it down into more steps.

As You Think, So You Are.

I asked John once about a cue he was describing that sounded very much like another cue he used for something completely different. "How does the horse sort it out?" I asked.

"As you think, so you are," he replied. "Because I'm thinking differently, the horse perceives me and the cue differently." It's all based on the premise that horses detect extremely subtle changes in humans, from changes in respiration and heart rate to dilated pupils, to the amount of tension in our muscles. The physical act of performing a cue is just part of the communication going on. The horse effectively reads a human's mind by reading his body.

> It's absolutely critical that you have in your mind a clear picture of what you want the horse to do.

This is another reminder of how important it is to have your head in the game when you work with horses. It's absolutely critical that you have in your mind a clear picture of what you want the horse to do and exactly what is an acceptable try from him. This is the first step to developing the timing and feel that great horsemen have.

John Lyons is an original and I think about his horse training principles often. His son, Josh, and his daughter, Brandi, are following in his footsteps.

Insights

- Fear comes from lack of control and dissipates when control returns.

- Giving a horse a job to do helps eliminate unwanted behavior.

- Lowering his head to the ground has a calming effect on a horse.

- A consistent positive reward for a correct response accelerates a horse's learning.

- A horse gives you attention when you show him you can move his feet.

- Having a plan with detailed steps aids in training a horse.

- Ours thoughts as well as our actions affect how horses perceive us.

TRY THIS

Be Certain Your Horse Will Do What You're Asking Him to Do

"The horse only understands what happens, not whether it is right or wrong," John Lyons says. John recommends that you never ask a horse to do something unless you are nearly certain he will actually try to do it. If he refuses, that refusal becomes a valid response in the horse's mind because it happened. It was real.

Before you ask your horse to do anything, ask yourself, "Do I really believe this horse is going to do this?" If you're not certain, either slow down your training or break the lesson into smaller steps that you're certain the horse can handle.

But even if you're sure the horse understands, he may still fail to try. If that happens, do not back off. Turn up the intensity of the request until there is some sort of try.

Failure to get a try, whether due to the horse not understanding or the trainer not being willing to turn up the heat enough, teaches the horse the wrong lesson.

26 On the Road to the Horse

An "Edutainment" Phenomenon
Is Born

Since 2003, I've been intimately involved with a very special annual event, Road to the Horse, originally known by its Spanish equivalent, *El Camino del Caballo*. It is a colt starting challenge, and the term itself requires some clarification.

Horse Breaking

It used to be that the process of getting a horse to accept a saddle, bridle, and rider was called *breaking* the horse. Often, but not always, it was a battle between the horse and the human. It could be exciting, but too often it was also violent, and one or both of the participants were hurt. Many horses actually died in the breaking process.

Breaking a horse pushed him deeply into survival mode. He would buck furiously in an attempt to get the predator—who was often egging him on by spurring him, spanking him with a quirt, and even fanning him with his hat—off his back. Eventually, the horse would wear himself out and stop fighting the rider. The common explanation was that the horse's

Breaking a horse floods him with sensory input that blasts right past his threshold of tolerance.

spirit had been broken. Historically, that method produced many usable horses, but it did not promote a partnership built on respect and trust between horse and human.

In scientific terms, breaking a horse floods him with sensory input that blasts right past his threshold of tolerance, causes fear, ignites his flight response, and keeps him in a reactive state of mind until sheer exhaustion forces him to give up the fight and submit. There is very little reason or opportunity for the horse to think while breaking is going on.

It's tempting to relate this to bucking events in rodeo, but they are very different. The rodeo bucking horse is an equine athlete with a job he has learned to do. He may have been bred for this specific purpose. He is respected, pampered, and protected. When he works, it is for eight seconds at a time. The last thing a rodeo stock contractor wants to do is break the spirit of such a horse.

Colt Starting

The horsemanship revolution that produced natural horsemanship also produced a different approach to preparing a horse to ride. "Breaking" has become, "breaking in" and carries the same connotation as breaking in a new pair of shoes or a new vehicle or a new employee. It means taking it easy in the beginning and gradually asking for more.

Horsemen who regularly start colts have developed highly efficient ways to do it.

Even more popular now is the term, "starting" the colt. A colt in this context simply means an untrained horse, male or female. Usually it's a young horse, from two to four years in age, but the term would still apply to an older horse that has never been trained to do a job.

Starting a colt is a high-level horsemanship skill because the goal is to create a partner instead of a slave, to instill respect without fear. Even so, it can still be dangerous, and horses can still act unpredictably. If there is no reason to hurry the process along, most colts can be fully started in a week's time, working an hour or less each day. But in the real world, there are always time constraints, so those horsemen

Road to the Horse shows how quickly a colt can be trained to comply with a rider's wishes.

who regularly start colts have developed highly efficient ways to do it, without sacrificing principle or end result.

The benchmark for riding a colt is thirty minutes. Dr. Billy Linfoot, veterinarian and polo hall-of-famer, was known for being able to ride a mustang bareback in just thirty minutes. Monty Roberts, an internationally known natural horseman and author, has performed hundreds of public demonstrations in which he has a colt accepting saddle, bridle, and rider in less than thirty minutes. This sort of demonstration just emphasizes how quickly the horse's confidence can be won. It does not show how quickly a colt can be trained to comply with a rider's wishes. Road to the Horse does.

The Competition

Each year, a small herd of colts—a *remuda*—is brought to the event from a particular ranch. The colts are as identical in breeding and conformation as possible. Typically, they are three- or four-year-old American Quarter Horses with performance horse bloodlines. They are the same gender, either all females or all geldings. Prior to the contest, the horses have been handled only for routine veterinary procedures. In some cases, they've been taught to lead, but never anything more than that.

> At the end of the event, the judges, along with everyone else, find out who won.

Each phase of the competition is judged on a point system. Judges are highly respected, veteran horsemen with no vested interest in the outcome. Their scorecards are picked up after each phase. When the scores are tallied at the end of the event, the judges, along with everyone else, find out who won.

One thing that has changed over the years is how the horses and trainers are matched up. In some years, the judges preselected the three most similar colts from the remuda and a drawing from a hat assigned each trainer to a horse. Another year, the judges selected two such horses for each trainer and the trainer drew a pair of horses, one of which he would select to train.

Yet another idea tried was to let the trainers choose their own horses from the remuda at large. The order of go was determined by a drawing from a hat. Doing this added another dimension to the challenge. Just how well could a trainer read a horse and predict how easily he could be taught to do the tasks required? It might mean setting aside the trainer's personal preferences in favor of expediency. The contest was all about getting the horse working willingly as quickly as possible without losing the horse's trust.

Most other aspects of the Road to the Horse format have remained the same. The event proper is spread over two days. Day One is a get-acquainted day. Each trainer performs a one-hour mini-clinic to introduce himself and his general training approach to the audience. These short presentations often contain an amazing amount of usable information, but mostly they are about getting to know the competitors. Day One also introduces the remuda of horses in a memorable way. To the strains of dramatic music, the horses are hustled into the arena by the boss wrangler and his helpers, and stirred up to get some interaction between them. It's exciting and emotional to watch for all of us horse lovers, but its real purpose is to allow the horses that will be used in the contest to be selected.

Just how well could a trainer read a horse and predict how easily he could be taught to do the tasks required?

Day One concludes with the first training session, done in matching 50-foot round pens. This first session was originally one hour. In 2007, it was extended to two hours to allow the training to progress a bit more slowly. With the extra hour of training time comes a mandatory ten-minute rest break. Judges' cards are picked up at the end of the session. On Day Two, the trainers and their assigned horses are put in different round pens than on Day One. This is to give the audience a different view and also to add one more variable—a change of scenery for the horses—to the challenge. Judges' scorecards are picked up at the conclusion of the round pen training and the pens are removed from the arena.

The Test

The Test comes next. The Test has required tasks and a freestyle component. With the exception of picking up all four feet, the required tasks are all done on the horse's back.

The horse is to be ridden in a straight line for 40 feet. He is to be ridden on the rail (at the outer edge of the arena) in both directions at a walk, trot, and canter. He is also to be stopped and backed up. Then comes the obstacle course, which generally includes weaving in and out of poles, walking through a narrow lane with 90-degree turns, stepping over a series of poles lying on the ground, walking across a plastic tarp, stepping over a pole suspended between two bales of hay, picking up a rope and twirling it over the horse's head, and finally, picking up a second rope attached to a log and pulling the log 15 feet.

The freestyle component of the test can be anything the trainer wants to do to show off his horse and the relationship the two of them have built. Usually it is a demonstration of how tolerant the horse is to stimuli that would have previously frightened him.

Again the judges' scorecards are collected, but this time the results for the entire competition are tallied. For each trainer, the high and low scores he received from judges in a particular category are discarded and the three remaining scores are averaged. In the end, the trainer with the highest score wins. One of the categories for which judges assign a score is the degree of difficulty that the horse repre- **The real judge is the audience.** sents. It's thus conceivable that a trainer working with a very difficult horse could outscore one working with an easier horse and getting more done. It's as fair a system as I can imagine and it is only tweaked when there is some way discovered that would make it even more fair.

The real judge of Road to the Horse is the audience, the people who see the event live and those who watch later. Tickets are sold out months in advance. A live webcast serves many of those who can't be there in person, and a professionally produced video is always available a few months after each event. As a group, the audience for Road to the Horse is more sophisticated than the average horse enthusiast. Most members are actively involved in training their own horses. Some are followers of one of the competitors.

I have served as emcee, host, and commentator for the past four Road to the Horse events. I'm deeply honored to serve in this capacity, and I put everything I have into it each year. My bird's eye view of what goes on in the pens—and my understanding of its implications—allows me to bring an extra dimension to the event for those watching. Still, I walk away with perhaps the greatest enrichment of anyone.

Road to the Horse is *edutainment*—a marriage of education and entertainment—at its best. It is the Super Bowl of colt starting. There are bright lights, music, action, moments of triumph and moments of failure, mistakes and missteps, suspense and comedy. Horse training is hard and often unpredictable, but it's also great fun and the good-natured barbs exchanged by the competitors, who are often friends outside the arena, provide some of the most memorable moments.

Road to the Horse is the Super Bowl of colt starting.

Because so many people have expressed interest in my thoughts on each of these events, I'll walk you through them and share what sticks out in my mind for each.

Insights

- The traditional method of breaking a horse's spirit in order to ride him is no longer necessary or desirable.

- Starting horses under saddle can be done as a competitive event without danger to horse or rider.

TRY THIS

Watch a Colt Starting Event

Every year, at ranches, horse farms, and public events around the world, young horses are started under saddle. The methods vary but most of them now seek to get the job done without physical or emotional trauma to the horse. The goal is to instill in the horse both respect and trust for the human, while establishing a system of communication between the two species. Observe this process as often as you can. Try to recognize the subtle changes in the horse's behavior and body language that signal a change in attitude.

27 **Road Trips**
The Formative Years of Road to the Horse

The predecessor to Road to the Horse was a documentary video on "horse whispering." It was co-produced by Tootie Bland, who went on to create Road to the Horse with her husband, Steven. The video sparked the idea of a training competition, struck a nerve with the public, and inspired me to get involved.

In a Whisper Challenge 2002—August 3, 2002

Contestants: Craig Cameron, Josh Lyons, Pat Parelli
Judges: Marion Buehler, Robert Moorhouse, Dale Segraves
Hosts and commentators: Sam Smith and Bob Tallman
Location: Sundance Square, Fort Worth, Texas

The competition featured in the documentary was a single two-and-a-half hour round pen training session, followed by a test. Through a drawing, each trainer was assigned a round pen containing two horses. He had ten minutes with which to become familiar with the horses and decide which one he wanted to train.

Like the colt starting challenges that would follow, this one saw a variety of training methods employed. Pat Parelli chose the more difficult of the two horses in his pen and spent a great deal of time flagging the horse with a long pole, trying to desensitize him, and then working a long line to sensitize the horse to pressure. When it came time for the Test, his horse was the least comfortable and did not perform well.

Craig Cameron generally made better progress with his horse, although the horse did buck hard when he was first saddled. One of the great moments of this event was when Craig loped his horse around the ring bridleless. Overall, Craig's Test went more smoothly than Pat's.

But it was Josh Lyons, who had already stepped out of the shadow of his father, John, who most impressed the judges. Unlike the other trainers, Josh got his horse into a bridle with a snaffle bit very early in the training session and utilized the bridle extensively in what followed. Although technically, Josh did not complete the Test because he did not canter his horse (saying, "This horse is not ready to canter"), he still won the contest based on the judges' decisions.

> Josh got his colt into a bridle with a snaffle bit very early in the training session.

I did not attend this event, but I did know about it ahead of time. Tootie's partner contacted me a week or so in advance to see about getting some publicity on my radio show, but it was too late to make that happen. A few months later, I received a VHS copy of the video.

Coincidentally, that tape arrived just as Diana and I were leaving for Parachute, Colorado, to do some audio recording and a bit of snowmobiling with John Lyons and his new bride, Jody. We sat in John's living room and watched the video together.

John saw it from a horse trainer's point of view, and also from the point of view of a proud father. Josh is a superb horse trainer, applying John's philosophy and methodology with the timing and feel of a natural athlete.

I saw the video with different eyes. The event had been hosted by veteran horse show announcer, Sam Smith. With a moment's notice, legendary rodeo announcer Bob Tallman had stepped in to assist as a personal favor to Tootie. As much as I respected both men, I felt they were out of their element. This was an exhibition of natural horsemanship, not a horse show or a rodeo. It was my area of interest and,

> This was an exhibition of natural horsemanship, not a horse show or a rodeo.

increasingly, my area of expertise. Although I'd never hosted a live event like this nor provided running commentary, I thought I might be able to add something valuable just the same. I decided right then and there, in John Lyons's living room, that I would throw my hat in the ring if a sequel came about.

Diana and I were very aware that this was a golden opportunity for me, a chance to redefine my role in the horse industry from simply a guy who asks questions to a guy who can provide intelligent analysis and lend a professional air to horse events.

Bob Costas blew me away with the kind of commentary he could spin off the top of his head.

Here I was, about to reinvent myself again. Fortunately, I had a role model: sports commentator, Bob Costas. From an Olympic triathalon to a World Series baseball game, Costas always has just the right thing to say, and he never breaks a sweat. I had the privilege of working with Bob once in my studio. He blew me away with the kind of commentary he could spin off the top of his head as he watched a video clip. Plus, he was a nice guy, and a real class act. It doesn't always turn out that way.

El Camino del Caballo 2003—December 12–13, 2003

Contestants: Clinton Anderson, Josh Lyons, Curt Pate
Judges: Robert Moorhouse, Jack Brainard, Dr. Robert M. Miller,
  Buster McLaury, Michael B. Richardson
Host and commentator: Rick Lamb
Location: Cowtown Coliseum, Fort Worth, Texas

After In a Whisper, the partners who produced the documentary went separate ways. Tootie and Steven Bland launched Road to the Horse, or as it was called the first year, *El Camino del Caballo*. Significant changes were made to the format. The competition was expanded to two days, took place indoors where an arena could be utilized for the Test, featured matched colts from a single ranch, and had a full set of rules for the benefit of both the trainers and the horses.

Tootie accepted my offer to host. Unfortunately, there wasn't a great turnout, due mostly to poor timing. Mid-December is just a tough time to bring out a crowd for anything, especially if they have to travel.

Curt appeared to be running away with the contest.

Locally, there was competition from a major cutting event. Video of the event suffered technical problems and the director abandoned the project when he saw how poorly his planning, especially regarding audio, had been. Still, Tootie managed to salvage enough of the video to document what had happened. People loved it in spite of its problems.

The training portion of the event had been expanded to one hour of round pen training on the first day and two hours on the second day. I remember distinctly how the tide turned in this event. On the first day, Curt Pate was amazing and seemed to get much more done than either Josh or Clinton. In fact, Curt appeared to be running away with the contest. It was a pleasure seeing him work.

Josh seemed to be struggling, trying this and that without much success. Maybe he had a plan but I couldn't see him working it.

Clinton was just the opposite; he had a detailed plan on index cards that he kept pulling out of his back pocket. In an earlier on-camera interview, I had asked the three trainers what, if anything, they would change in their usual colt starting method to suit this timed event. Only Clinton had a plan.

With just fifteen minutes of his time remaining, Clinton asked that the judging begin.

During the second day of round pen training, however, Clinton seemed to be lagging behind the other two trainers. In fact, with less than thirty minutes left in the two-hour session, he was still concentrating on groundwork and had not mounted his horse. When he finally did, the horse progressed very quickly, and at the end of the second round pen session, it seemed to be anybody's game.

Clinton drew to ride his Test first. The rules now allowed the contestant to use a portion of his twenty-five-minute Test for additional training. It was up to him to indicate to me when he wanted judging of the Test to start.

Clinton used this to his advantage, spending another ten minutes walking his horse around the perimeter and doing more groundwork, talking to the audience the entire time. Finally, with just fifteen minutes of his time remaining, Clinton asked that the judging begin. He walked, trotted, and cantered his horse smoothly around the perimeter of the arena and negotiated the obstacle course with no problem.

He could have stopped right there and been in a great position to win the event. Instead, Clinton moved immediately into his freestyle, which he had obviously planned just as carefully. With his colt standing rock steady, Clinton slowly got to his feet on the horse's back. Although Pat Parelli had done this at the In a Whisper Challenge, he had done so at the edge of the arena, steadying himself on the framework of the gate. Clinton did it in the wide-open arena. To further prove how comfortable his horse had become, Clinton waved a kangaroo hide and then a yellow rain slicker over his head. The horse remained steady.

Clinton cracked the stock whip over the horse's head while standing on his back.

For his grand finale, Clinton took the stock whip out of his belt and began cracking it repeatedly over the horse's head while continuing to stand on his back. At last, the horse took a step and Clinton jumped down, promptly crawling under the horse's belly in one final demonstration of how calm and quiet the colt had become.

Josh rode his Test next. His horse performed unevenly and there was still a lot of resistance coming from the gelding. Josh completed the rail and obstacle portion of the Test, but did not canter his horse, saying, "You guys know me from last time; I'm not a big loper on a first time ride." It was a reference to having won the first event without meeting this requirement. He also declined to do any freestyle.

"I want to honor my granddad, and I think my granddad would say this colt has had enough for the day."

Curt rode his Test last, In general, his horse was more responsive on the Test and readily took the lope when asked. Curt also declined to do anything for the freestyle, saying, with obvious emotion in his voice, "I want to honor my granddad, and I think my granddad would say this colt has had enough for the day." He received a warm round of applause from the audience as he led his horse out of the arena.

When the judges' scores were tallied, Clinton Anderson was named the winner.

Road to the Horse 2005—March 5–6, 2005

Contestants: Clinton Anderson, Craig Cameron, Van Hargis
Judges: Robert Moorhouse, Jack Brainard, Dr. Robert M. Miller,
Mike Kevil, Cherry Hill
Host and commentator: Rick Lamb
Location: Tennessee Miller Coliseum, Murfreesboro, Tennessee

The next three Road to the Horse competitions took place at the Tennessee Miller Coliseum in Murfreesboro, Tennessee. Being more centrally located and getting it away from the holiday season helped drive

It is not a sign of failure when a horse bucks.

up attendance. But the biggest reason for the increase in attendance was Clinton. As returning champion, he promoted the event tirelessly on his television program and tour stops. The stands were full and no one went away disappointed.

The horses were three-year-old fillies instead of geldings as in the previous two events. As before, they came from the same ranch, had been raised identically, and had virtually no training on them.

All three trainers had their share of trouble with their horse. Van Hargis had a gorgeous, fine-boned gray mare. She was very athletic and very suspicious. It took Van a long time to gain her trust and when he finally did, he dropped to his knees and thanked the good Lord in what turned out to be one of the seminal images from the event.

Both Craig and Clinton had bigger fillies that were lazier, pushier, and more disrespectful. Both men would have to turn up the heat to get through to these horses.

This event had a fair amount of bucking in it. I have learned from being around these veteran colt starters that bucking when a horse is first saddled is not the big deal it might seem to the rest of us. If a horse can be started without bucking, so much the better, but it is not a sign of failure when a horse bucks. It is simply an expression of the horse's need for self-preservation, as Tom Dorrance might put it.

Clinton followed the same plan he had used to win the previous year. However, this time, he added a leaf blower, a chainsaw (minus the chain) and pistols firing blanks to his desensitizing arsenal.

A memorable moment occurred near the end of the second day of training when Clinton's filly became particularly obstinate and refused to move forward under saddle. Clinton went back to something the horse was willing to do, dismounted and ended his training session early.

I learned an important lesson from that: it is always better to end a training session on your terms before the horse ends it by shutting down.

> It is always better to end a training session on your terms before the horse ends it by shutting down.

Clinton was named winner for the second consecutive year, and announced that he would not return the following year to defend his title. That meant an entirely new field of contestants, one that was significantly different from those in the past. Excitement began building immediately. Then Fate stepped in and changed Road to the Horse forever.

Insights

- You will get better results in training horses if you have a plan.
- Creating a solid foundation through groundwork will make the riding go better.
- A slower start may prove more effective.
- It is not a problem if the horse bucks the first time he's saddled; it is a problem if he bucks every time he's saddled.

TRY THIS

Do Groundwork Every Day

Groundwork is not only for starting a horse. Nor is it only for use in a round pen. Every time you are in contact with your horse, you have an opportunity to perform groundwork with him. When you halter your horse, ask him to back up a few steps, then ask him to disengage his hindquarters (cross one hind leg in front of the other as he moves his rear end away from you). When you lead him from one place to another, vary your speed, and stop now and then. Require that the horse keep pace with you, with his head even with your elbow. If he surges forward or falls behind, or crowds you, stop and school him. Ask your horse to walk past you and into his stall or the wash rack. Use everyday opportunities to test your horse's understanding of ground commands and his willingness to obey them.

28 Queen of the Road
Softness and Lightness in Action

A Death in the Family

The months leading up to Road to the Horse 2006 were very sad. Co-producer Steven Bland, top hand, stuntman, movie wrangler, rodeo champion, and most importantly, husband to Tootie, died unexpectedly. It took a great deal of courage and determination for Tootie to go on

> Somehow, the right words were there when I needed them.

without him, but she knew beyond any doubt that he would have wanted her to continue building their dream.

I'll never forget walking out in front of that packed arena to start the event and hoping I would find the words to eulogize Steven. I knew it was right to remember him, but I also felt strongly that he would want the event to be a celebration of the horse and not a time of sadness.

I rehearsed nothing ahead of time. Somehow, the right words were there when I needed them. Tootie was touched and later she told me, with tears in her eyes, "It was perfect."

This year, the field was increased to four trainers. Craig Cameron and Van Hargis returned, and there were two trainers I didn't know: Martin Black and Stacy Westfall.

Martin Black is a top hand, a professional colt starter from a long line of fine horsemen. On the

> The colt gave a couple good bucks that a lesser cowboy could not have handled.

first day of round pen training, he seemed to be walking away with the

Road to the Horse 2006—February 25–26, 2006

Contestants: Martin Black, Craig Cameron, Van Hargis,
Stacy Westfall

Judges: Robert Moorhouse, Jack Brainard, Dr. Robert M. Miller,
Mike Kevil, Toni Warvell

Host and commentator: Rick Lamb

Location: Tennessee Miller Coliseum, Murfreesboro, Tennessee

contest. A rule change allowed a trained saddle horse to be taken into the round pen with the colt and Martin made maximum use of that. Within a few minutes he had haltered his colt and was leading him around from the back of his saddle horse. He was also the first to mount his horse and had him negotiating some obstacles in his pen long before anyone else.

Martin's lead evaporated during the test on the second day, however. In the wide-open arena without his buddy horse for security, the colt was worried and unresponsive. When Martin insisted the horse move forward, he gave a couple good bucks that a lesser cowboy could not have handled. Martin kept his seat but lost his big black hat.

Stacy Westfall seemed a bit out-of-place among these rugged cowboys. She is a phenomenal rider best known for World Championship-winning freestyle reining routines done bareback and bridleless.

If Martin was the clear favorite on Day One, Stacy was the clear underdog. By the end of the first day, she had barely gotten a halter on her horse. Still she had been very methodical in laying a foundation with the horse

> The horse fought the hobbles, thrashing about and finally falling to the ground.

and I had the feeling she would reap the benefit on Day Two. She did. The horse, which she later announced she was purchasing and had named "Popcorn," showed remarkable confidence in Stacy on Day Two. The round pen training progressed quickly and the Test was really amazing.

Craig had a difficult horse—probably the most difficult of the four—and at one point, he tried some hobbles on the horse's front legs. I had interviewed Craig once in front of a live audience on his use of hobbles and

I knew his commitment to their proper, safe, traditional use. This horse fought the hobbles, thrashing about and finally falling to the ground. Some audience members were quick to judge Craig's decision and he suffered some not-so-kind heckling.

Van's horse was nervous and worried, and had a distinct problem with anything coming near his back legs. Van spent most of his time trying to deal with this problem and spent little time on the horse's back.

When all was said and done, the winner by the judge's decision, and by audience acclaim, was Stacy Westfall. She proved that a petite, feminine woman could also start colts, and do it well.

It was planned ahead of time that during the award ceremony, I would invite Clinton into the arena to publicly inquire about whether he might return to compete the following year. He congratulated Stacy and announced that he would return. About that time, my cell phone rang. It was Chris Cox challenging both Stacy and Clinton to meet him for a battle of champions. Although Chris had never appeared at Road to the Horse, he had won other colt-starting events. Of course, the call was staged and it came off beautifully. We planted the seeds for the mother of all colt starting contests, Road to the Horse 2007.

Road to the Horse 2007—March 2–3, 2007

Contestants: Clinton Anderson, Chris Cox, Stacy Westfall
Judges: Robert Moorhouse, Jack Brainard, Dr. Robert M. Miller, Mike Kevil, Toni Warvell, Lindy Burch (alternate)
Host and commentator: Rick Lamb
Location: Tennessee Miller Coliseum, Murfreesboro, Tennessee

By 2006, my television show was in the works and I was working on my third book. Regretfully, I gave notice to Clinton that I could not host his tour in the coming year. Still, both the public and other clinicians associated me with him. I didn't mind then and I don't mind now—he's a great horseman and a great friend—but I was surprised at how inaccurate those perceptions were.

During summer of that same year, Diana and I visited Chris Cox's ranch in Mineral Wells, Texas, for the dual purpose of advising him on

Little did I know that Chris had some doubts about me.

his sound system and videotaping a ranch tour with him for our TV show. Chris was gracious and re-laxed, and the resulting television program was one

of our best in season one. Little did I know that Chris had some doubts about me.

Road to the Horse 2007 was the biggest event yet in this series. The 5,000 permanent seats at Tennessee Miller Coliseum were sold out sev-eral months before the event. Portable bleachers to accommodate 1,500 additional people were secured and those sold out quickly, too. Then a web cast was arranged and another 1,200 people signed up for that. All together, the event was seen live by more than 7,700 people.

The first day of the competition was electric. With so many people in the stands and watching on their computers, we all felt a bit more pres-sure than usual. As in previous years, the first and second days of Road to the Horse had very different outcomes.

The round pen session for Day One had been expanded to nearly two hours, with a mandatory rest break in the middle. Clinton used the time

Clinton realized he had started something he couldn't finish.

for groundwork and desensitizing his horse to gunshots, a clanging cowbell, a string of brightly colored marine buoys, and shiny streamers tied

to the horse's legs. At the end of the session, he decided to ride the horse. He later admitted that was a mistake.

The horse objected and would not move out as Clinton wanted him to. Turning up the heat a bit caused the horse to become more agitated. Clinton realized that he had started something he couldn't finish in the time that remained. He searched for a positive note to end on, finally found one, dismounted and made it through his gate before the buzzer sounded, ending round one.

Stacy seemed to be on a similar course to her previous year's perfor-mance; she was busy laying a foundation. This horse, however, was more difficult than Popcorn had been.

To the casual observer, Chris was getting the least done with his horse.

Unlike Clinton and Stacy, who had readily achieved "join-up," that moment when the horse signals he'd rather be *with* the trainer than away from the trainer, Chris's horse was having none of that. The horse's body language remained tense, even though he was responding to Chris's groundwork commands. Time and again, Chris took the pressure off the horse and stepped back, turned, and walked away, trying to

> The horse watched Chris intently with his mouth clamped shut and his muscles tense.

draw the horse into a join-up moment. The horse refused to be drawn in. He watched Chris intently with his mouth clamped shut and his muscles tense, clearly unwilling to place his trust in this human.

During all of this, I provided running commentary from the space between the three pens, dividing my comments as evenly as I could. At the end of the day, we all relaxed in the VIP lounge above the arena, where a surprise party for Bob Miller's eightieth birthday was to take place. Chris Cox approached me with a serious look on his face.

"Nice job in there today," I said.

"Thanks. Listen, Rick, I have something I want to say to you," he replied. "Going into this deal, I thought you might be Clinton's guy."

I said nothing, trying not to act surprised.

"But after today," he continued, "I can see that you're not. You're really trying to be fair out there and I appreciate it."

I could tell Chris was speaking from the heart.

"Well, Chris," I grinned as I shook his hand, "I'm just happy to be part of this."

Day Two began with the usual opening ceremony. Country star Trent Willmon sang the National Anthem and John Payne, the One-Arm Bandit, did his amazing act once more. John is a phenomenal rider and entertainer who races around the arena on a horse or a mule, cracking a bullwhip and driving a variety of livestock to the top of his long, custom-built horse trailer. He does it all without the use of one of his arms, the result of an accident during his career as an electrical lineman. On several occasions, I've had to stand my ground in the arena with John's horses, mules, buffalo, and longhorn steer thundering straight at me.

The round pen session of Day Two had some excitement. Stacy uncovered a problem with her horse striking with his front feet when she waved her training stick in front of him. She lost a lot of time trying to overcome it. One of the judges later told me that he felt she was actually making the problem worse. At any rate, Stacy forged forward and rode her horse in the pen. In the Test, it became clear that the horse had much to learn. With her usual positive attitude, Stacy stuck it out and finished.

> Stacy uncovered a problem with her horse striking with his front feet.

Clinton's second round pen session had one heart-stopping moment. After continuing his desensitizing plan by firing pistols loaded with blanks and cracking his Aussie bullwhip, Clinton asked his colt to do some more groundwork. It was nothing new for the colt, but when he refused and Clinton turned up the heat, the colt went ballistic, charging Clinton with murder in his heart. Clinton sidestepped the charge and immediately went back to his groundwork, using the momentum of the horse's sudden movement to his advantage.

Later, when Clinton was riding the horse, he ran into that resistance again and gradually turned up the heat on the horse, using a dressage whip across the hindquarters with increasing intensity to get movement from the horse. What followed was the most serious bucking Clinton had endured in the saddle at Road to the Horse. Some voices from the audience rang out in criticism. Clinton's Test went relatively smoothly and he capped it off as he had in previous years, by standing on the horse's back, firing guns and cracking a whip.

Chris picked up where he left off with his horse. Still, there was no join-up. However, the horse became more willing to do Chris's bidding, either from the ground or in the saddle. Chris showed remarkable patience with his horse, supported him through every move, and kept pressure at just the right level. The Test went smoothly, with Chris's horse showing good willingness to move out when asked. At the end of the compulsory portion of the Test, Chris stood on his horse's back, the traditional demonstration of the horse's confidence in the rider.

The most dramatic moment of the competition came next. After finishing his Test early and announcing that he had nothing fancy to show for his freestyle, Chris dismounted, draped the reins over his horse's neck, and walked away, heading toward the far end of the arena. He literally gave the horse his freedom. Instead of running off, the horse turned and followed him, head down, ears forward, a classic and perfect example of join-up. The crowd went crazy. That moment was a real testament to the power of empathetic, psychological horse training. A few minutes later, when the judges' scores were tallied, Chris Cox was named the winner.

> That moment was a real testament to the power of empathetic, psychological horse training.

Good sportsmanship has always been evident at Road to the Horse and this year it was particularly true. Clinton and Stacy were genuinely happy for Chris. We all were.

Road to the Horse 2008—March 1–2, 2008

Contestants: Chris Cox, Tommy Garland, Ken McNabb, Mystery Trainer
Judges: To Be Determined
Host and commentator: Rick Lamb
Location: Tennessee Miller Coliseum, Murfreesboro, Tennessee

At this writing, Road to the Horse 2008 is several months in the future. It will feature four trainers, including returning champion Chris Cox, Ken McNabb, and Tommy Garland. The fourth trainer is being kept a secret until the night before the competition begins. This has led to much speculation about who it might be. Several people have guessed that it will be me. I'm flattered, of course, but I will need to start many more colts before being qualified for something like that. I can say this: the fourth trainer is a top horseman (which, of course, could be a woman) with plenty of experience starting colts. I will be there in my usual role, outside the round pens, with microphone in hand.

The Welfare of the Horse

I'd like to make one final comment about Road to the Horse. I can assure you that everyone associated with this event is a true horse lover. The commitment to the welfare of the horse starts at the top and permeates every level. Yet there are times during this event when horses seem to be handled roughly. How can this be?

Trainers who have gotten the job done with a lighter touch have been rewarded.

I wouldn't presume to second-guess the trainers or the judges, who are themselves fine horsemen. The rules of the event make excessive roughness grounds for penalties and even disqualification. Yet a penalty has never been given, nor has any trainer been disqualified. To me, this says that the judges haven't felt that any trainer has crossed the line. By the same token, trainers who have gotten the job done with a lighter touch have been rewarded.

The key realization on my journey has been that *each horse, each human, and each moment is unique*. Thus, I simply don't judge anymore. I observe, think, try to learn from what I see, and hope that I can bring it all together to make the best possible deal for the horse and for me if I'm ever in a similar situation.

Insights

- Natural horsemanship can be exciting.
- Starting a colt can proceed without join-up.
- Steady, persistent, sensitive handling can pay big dividends.
- In training, one must always adapt to fit the situation.

TRY THIS

Explain Natural Horsemanship

Nothing clarifies your own understanding of a subject better than trying to explain it to someone else. Do this with natural horsemanship. Explain what it means, where its value lies, how it differs from other approaches. Put it in your own words.

29 Television
Making the Most of Mass Communication

My first appearance on television was in the sixties. My cousins and I were in the audience of a local kids' program. I remember two things about the experience: how different the set was from how it looked on television, and how terrified I was that I would be singled out by the camera, or worse, by someone with a microphone. It was a particularly inauspicious start for someone who now makes his living on camera.

> I was terrified that I would be singled out by the camera.

Playing in rock bands through high school and college helped. It got me used to being in front of an audience. My radio show made me comfortable with talking extemporaneously and my live appearances at horse events got me accustomed to doing both at the same time. But doing it all on camera was taking this performance thing to another level. Fortunately, Diana was there to help me.

Before Diana and I got married, she was a well-known commercial actress and did a great deal of on-camera work, literally hundreds of TV commercials and corporate videos, plus a handful of feature films. One of the skills she had picked up along the way was teaching someone—anyone—how to perform on camera. It's why she's such a good director today.

Live on RFD-TV

My first experience actually hosting a television show was when Clinton

Anderson asked me to host a special live version of *Downunder Horsemanship®*, his one-hour television program on RFD-TV. It took place at an impressive video production facility in Nashville called North-Star Studios. Although RFD-TV had its corporate offices in Omaha, Nebraska, NorthStar was the operational hub and satellite uplink for the network.

Because I had spent so much time in production facilities, I was instantly at home at NorthStar. On the day of the show we arrived early in the afternoon to iron out all the details of the live broadcast scheduled for that evening. Then we had time to go back to our hotel and relax before the broadcast.

When we arrived back at NorthStar, we were ushered to our dressing rooms, where someone had kindly put my name on the door, just like a real star. Next stop was makeup, where any imperfections in our skin tone or complexion were instantly erased. By the time we were on the set, we had been immersed in the ambiance and thinking about what was to come for several hours.

You've probably seen the small earpiece a broadcaster wears on camera. Mine connected me to the director of the program, the guy who controlled the cameras, the callers, the music, the graphics, the video clips—literally everything about the way the program came off to viewers—from another part of the building. My job was to host the show and act like I was the one in charge, even though I was getting direction through the earpiece. As it turned out, it was a bigger acting job than I expected.

It was a bigger acting job than I expected.

Earlier in the day, we had all gone over Clinton's plan for the show. It was well thought out and allowed for casual conversation between Clinton and me, as well as time for callers to ask Clinton questions that he would answer on the air. Video clips of Clinton working with horses in various situations had been gathered and made ready to supplement what we discussed on the air. I had the plan firmly in mind and notes in my lap, just in case.

When the show went on the air, I went into my "zone." It's something I've learned to do over the years. There's a rush of adrenaline, I have more

energy, and I think more clearly. Anyone who does live performances of
any kind knows exactly what I mean.

For the first half of the show, things went pretty much according to plan, but then the director
started changing things on the fly, deciding to put

> **The director started changing things on the fly instead of sticking to the plan.**

additional callers on the air, instead of sticking to the plan. It rattled me at
first, but I recovered quickly. To make matters worse, there was no clock
in my line of sight. All I could do was sneak a look at my watch now and
then to keep track of where we were in the show.

Somehow I kept my cool, Clinton rolled with the punches, and we got
through the hour in fine shape. I got good marks on my performance and
planted the seed with Patrick Gotsch, owner of RFD-TV, that I might
have a future on the network.

Clinton and I did the same thing again a year or so later. Again, the
show went smoothly and I received many kind kudos for my hosting.
This was something I knew I could do.

Taking *The Horse Show* to Television

Several years earlier, Diana and I had developed a concept for our own
TV show built around my interviews, but at the time there was no prov-
en way of getting a television program to horse people. RFD-TV changed
all that. By creating a network specifically for rural America and deliver-
ing it by satellite, Patrick had tapped into a huge, loyal, and horse-friendly
audience. Still, even after hosting Clinton's live shows, the idea of having
my own TV program lay idle in my brain until I received a phone call that
changed everything.

The phone call came in early 2006 and was from Rick Swan, who was
interested in national radio advertising for Daily72, a new mineral product for horses. I had no openings for new advertisers at the time, but I
agreed to a meeting anyway. It was one of the smarter things I've done.

At the meeting, I learned about the company and offered various suggestions on how they might use audio in their marketing. As we were
winding down, Rick asked me what I wanted to do in the future. Without
missing a beat, I said, "Television." That sparked a lively discussion of the

possibility of Daily72 sponsoring a television version of *The Horse Show with Rick Lamb*.

I knew that Rick Swan was a sharp marketer with lots of experience and contacts in the horse industry. I felt he could generate some excitement about the show, not only with his boss but with other sponsors.

Our first season was sold out, a feat almost unheard of.

I decided to swing for the fences. I put together a production budget that included buying air time on RFD-TV, travel, editing, shipping and all the incidentals I knew could eat a show alive if you weren't careful.

Daily72 signed on, and was joined by the Farnam Companies, Fort Dodge Animal Health, Wahl Clipper, Valley Vet Supply, and Ritchie Industries. Our first season was sold out, a feat almost unheard of, and eerily reminiscent of my start in radio. It was clear to me that we were meant to do this.

The logistics of shooting and editing the show fell into place quickly. Diana became the primary videographer and we began taking a large padded bag of video equipment on all our travels to expos and other horse events. We found interesting people and stories to cover everywhere we went. Diana soon became the roughcut editor, as well, assembling the basic flow of each program. Finish editing went to Jay Casmirri, an old friend of mine who had expanded his formidable talents in graphic design into a career as a fine video editor. For several years, he had also been my partner in a music duo called, "The Blenderz").

The show employed a magazine format with a great deal of variety. Our first program, the pilot that sold both the sponsors and RFD-TV, was typical. I learned to ride a cutting horse from world champion Al Dunning. We also got a look at some state of the art equine dentistry and a farrier contest.

The outakes were mostly me getting tongue-tied. People loved it.

One thing I felt would go over big was showing outakes while the credits rolled by at the end of the show. In the first program, viewers saw me nearly come off the cutting horse when he made a sudden move. As the season progressed, the outakes were mostly me getting tongue-tied. People loved it. I think it somehow endeared me to them and when I met them, it always gave them something to rib me about, which really helped to break the ice.

Our second program of season one featured me learning to play horse soccer and riding in a celebrity cutting contest, where I took second place and went home with a big bronze trophy. Our third program was a research piece on nineteenth-century horseman, John Rarey. It became the prototype for our historical segments. We also did a ranch tour, a personality profile with a country music star, a cowboy mounted shooting event, and a variety of interviews with interesting people on interesting subjects. We wanted the show to be eclectic and unpredictable, and that's exactly what it was.

My moments of triumph and disappointment are shared with thousands of people.

While each person's journey from human to Horseman is unique and personal, mine is different in yet another way. It is a public journey. My moments of triumph and disappointment are shared with thousands of people, most of whom I don't know. This has its upside and its downside.

On the downside, I don't get to fail in private. If I try something new with a horse, chances are a camera is rolling. People tend to put me on better, more athletic horses than I would otherwise have the opportunity to ride. If I'm struggling with a concept, chances are I'm talking about it on the radio, or writing about it.

The upside is that all of this has intensified and accelerated the pace of my journey. I don't get to stay inside my comfort zone. I have deadlines to meet, programs to create, and books to write. I have reasons every day to get up and push forward on my journey at the fastest pace I can handle.

Horsemanship is a mental pursuit just as much as it is a physical pursuit. For me, radio, television, and books are just as integral to my mental journey as touching a horse is to my physical journey.

30 **The Journey Continues**
Remembering What Is Important

My mind is filled with many things as I go forward on my journey. There's excitement, optimism, pride in what I've learned, humility about all I have left to learn, eagerness to help horses and people when I can, and of course, gratitude for being blessed with purpose in my life. Here are some of the things I want to keep in mind.

- **Keep learning**

The more I learn, the more I realize there is to learn. The process of learning is, by its very nature, humbling. If I continue to learn, I can be fairly certain I will not fall victim to arrogance. Keeping alive my hunger for knowledge is the best thing I can do for my horses and for my fellow man.

- **Do not judge**

This also is a byproduct of learning. Without being inside another person's skin, it is very difficult to fully understand the choices a person makes. Variables swirl about us that make every passing instant unique. Still, there is right and wrong. All I can expect of anyone is to do the right thing, as they perceive it, in every moment. That is what I require of myself.

- **Choose the battles**

There will be conflicts with horses and people that are simply not worth fighting. The trick is getting so good at reading a situation that I know when I can win a battle and when it is best to not even start it. Especially with a horse, a battle lost is worse than a battle avoided. Horses learn from every encounter they have with me.

- **Find balance**

The great horseman Xenophon wrote in 360 B.C. "Neither horse nor man likes anything in the world that is excessive." This timeless principle of moderation is remarkably simple. It's like standing in the middle on a seesaw. I have stability there. Balance is another way of describing it, the balancing of opposing ideas or forces. The need to find balance is a constant companion on this journey.

- **Be patient but productive**

Patience is certainly a noble quality for a human to have, yet even patience can be carried to an extreme. It must be balanced against productivity. There are times when having boundless patience with a horse or a human gives them no reason to try. Patience can easily slip into complacency, satisfaction with mediocrity or lack of progress. The great horsemen I have seen have a way of urging a horse to try with steady, deliberate, measured pressure. When they seem to have endless patience, it's really a matter of them seeing progress that others don't.

- **Do not be overly affectionate**

It's good to show affection to a horse, but I need to hold some of it back for rewarding the horse. Lavishing praise on a horse just for being a horse makes praise meaningless. Too much affection can also be interpreted by the horse as submissiveness. I need to maintain some dignity, no matter how much I love my horse. And always remember, the thing a horse appreciates most of all is simply being left alone.

- **Be a leader but not a bully**

I do not need to assert my leadership constantly around a horse. That comes very close to bullying. I will not tolerate disrespect from a horse but neither will dare him to disrespect me. That is setting him up to fail. I want it to be easy for the horse to respect my leadership.

- **Have confidence without arrogance**

I want my competence to be displayed to the world and to my horse as confidence, not arrogance. Arrogance is trying too hard. Arrogance is demanding that others take notice. Arrogance has an element of conceit to it. Most of all, arrogance masks underlying self-doubt. The truly competent person does not need to brag or strut. Confidence is quiet and strong.

- **Balance consistency and variety**

Consistency is desirable in how I use cues with my horse and how I enforce the rules. Consistency is not so desirable when it means every training session is the same. Variety in the experiences we have together is absolutely essential.

- **Get the job done as easily as possible**

I want to always observe the horseman's golden rule: "Be as gentle as possible and as firm as necessary" but I want to add to it, "to get the job done." There is purpose to working with a horse. It is with that goal of productivity in mind that I observe the golden rule.

- **Work toward subtlety**

I want to be absolutely clear in what I expect of the horse, but as time goes on, I want him to be able to read me as I read him. I should be able to be increasingly subtle with my cues as time goes on. If I can't, I'm doing something wrong.

- **Be an open-minded skeptic**

I don't know what I don't know, so becoming dogmatic and rigid in my beliefs is just plain foolish. I want to be open-minded to new ideas but temper it with skepticism. I want to be neither closed-minded nor gullible.

- **My behavior matters more than my species**

I am a predator because my species eats other animals. A horse is prey because his species is eaten. This distinction is only marginally useful because it doesn't take into account the behavior that each of us exhibits at a given time. If I am a benevolent leader, offer love and support to a horse, does it matter that I'm a predator by birth? By the same token, does it matter that a horse is a prey animal when he bites, kicks, or strikes a human? Behavior in the moment trumps a creature's position in the cycle of nature, and behavior can be changed. I want to balance my behavior between extremes of aggressiveness and passiveness as the situation dictates, always with the goal of being a loving leader to my horse.

- **Be in touch with the "other" me**

I must not be afraid of societal stereotypes regarding masculine and feminine behavior. I must give my horse what he needs in the moment, whether it is feminine nurturing or masculine strength.

- **Recognize "good enough"**

Nothing is perfect in life. The trick is knowing when I've reached "good enough." One of the key dangers in working with horses is going too far, striving too hard for perfection. Usually people get into trouble by not stopping soon enough. There is always another day, and the good horseman develops a sense about when he's reached a place where he and the horse can end on a positive note. As Tom Dorrance said, "If you end at a good place, then next time your horse will be that good or maybe a little better. If you end at a bad place, then next time the horse will probably be worse."

By the time you read this, I will have had countless more experiences and insights that are helping me along. My journey will never end. If others call me a Horseman, I will accept the compliment graciously, but my horses are the real judges. They tell me every day, "You're not quite there yet, Rick, but you keep on trying. We appreciate the effort."

I hope my horses and I see you down the trail.